www.wadsworth.com

wadsworth.com is the World Wide Web site for Wadsworth Publishing Company and is your direct source to dozens of online resources.

At *wadsworth.com* you can find out about supplements, demonstration software, and student resources. You can also send e-mail to many of our authors and preview new publications and exciting new technologies.

wadsworth.com
Changing the way the world learns®

Daily Planning for Today's Classroom

A Guide for Writing Lesson and Activity Plans

Kay M. Price
Karna L. Nelson

Woodring College of Education
Western Washington University

Wadsworth Publishing Company
I(T)P® An International Thomson Publishing Company

Belmont, CA • Albany, NY • Boston • Cincinnati • Johannesburg • London • Madrid• Melbourne
Mexico City • New York • Pacific Grove, CA • Scottsdale, AZ • Singapore • Tokyo • Toronto

Education Editor: Dianne Lindsay
Assistant Editor: Tangelique Williams
Marketing Manager: Becky Tollerson
Project Editor: Heidi Marschner
Print Buyer: Barbara Britton
Permissions Editor: Bob Kauser
Cover Design: Norman Baugher
Printer: The Mazer Corporation

For more information, contact Wadsworth Publishing Company, 10 Davis Drive, Belmont, CA 94002, or
electronically at http://www.wadsworth.com

International Thomson Publishing Europe
Berkshire House
168-173 High Holborn
London, WC1V 7AA, United Kingdom

Nelson ITP, Australia
102 Dodds Street
South Melbourne
Victoria 3205 Australia

Nelson Canada
1120 Birchmount Road
Scarborough, Ontario
Canada M1K 5G4

International Thomson Publishing Southern Africa
Building 18, Constantia Square
138 Sixteenth Road, P.O. Box 2459
Halfway House, 1685 South Africa

International Thomson Editores
Seneca, 53
Colonia Polanco
11560 México D.F. México

International Thomson Publishing Asia
60 Albert Street
#15-01 Albert Complex
Singapore 189969

International Thomson Publishing Japan
Hirakawa-cho Kyowa Building, 3F
2-2-1 Hirakawa-cho, Chiyoda-ku
Tokyo 102, Japan

ISBN 0-534-34917-X

Dedication

To Our Moms

Table of Contents

Preface

TO THE INSTRUCTOR

This book has been written for preservice teachers preparing for careers in general education or special education. It can be used to supplement initial instruction on the planning and delivery of lessons and activities. It can also be used as a review and guide for practicum students and student teachers.

We have written this book because of the common problems we have encountered, over the years, in our experiences with hundreds of practicum students and student teachers. Just like young students, preservice teachers cannot automatically transfer what they have learned to real life situations. In the real classroom, students seem to forget what they had learned from their training, while they scramble to survive. For example, while coping with the assignment of how to teach spelling to a particular group of sixth graders tomorrow at two o'clock, much of what they had learned about making instructional decisions is forgotten. They often simply try to copy what their cooperating teacher does or what the instructor's manual says.

Obviously, this text is not alone going to solve the serious and chronic problem of ensuring that preservice teachers transform theory into practice. However, we believe that it will help through its emphasis on writing rationales and detailed plans that reflect important steps in the decision-making process. Figuring out *what* to teach is beyond the scope of this book, even though we recognize that decisions on *how* to teach are affected by what one is teaching. Education students, typically, take many courses which focus on content and methods, and this text is not meant to take their place. Practicum students and student teachers often have no choice about the curriculum. They are being directed by a supervising teacher who has already made curriculum decisions. However, they are asked to make decisions about how to teach and that is the focus of this text.

Another problem with novice teachers is that they forget to teach. They are eager to involve children in learning and like to use exciting and creative approaches. However, they have trouble distinguishing between those occasions when students need the opportunity to practice and develop what they know and when students need to be directly taught new facts, concepts, and strategies. In their eagerness to be innovative, they plan fun activities but are unable to express what they want students to learn or why. Frequently, when they plan and teach lessons, they advance to providing student practice before they have taught enough to enable students to be successful with the practice. Novice teachers may select teaching methods based on their own interests or emerging "styles" rather than on the needs of their students. For these reasons, we make a distinction between activities and lessons, based on their purposes, and suggest different types of planning decisions for each. This distinction may be unnecessary for experienced teachers, but novice teachers find it helpful. In addition, accountability for teaching so that students learn is emphasized through a focus on clear objectives and evaluation of learning.

This book does not attempt to describe all models of teaching. The intention is to describe several rather straightforward models necessary for beginning teachers — e.g., direct instruction, structured discovery. More complex models — e.g., cooperative learning and inquiry — are not described, except as strategies or methods which can be incorporated within lessons or activities.

An important focus of this book is on planning for classes that include students with diverse learning needs. We believe that this comprises all classes in today's schools. Regardless of their intention to be general education or special education teachers, the fact is that all preservice teachers must be prepared to teach students at risk and students with disabilities. In addition, all preservice teachers need to be prepared to teach students from a variety of cultural backgrounds. We attempt to address the diversity issue by emphasizing the planning of lessons and activities, which include a variety of strategies intended to make it more likely that all students can learn. In programs which pair general education student teachers and special education student teachers, this book can provide a format for joint planning.

The text is divided into eleven chapters and an appendix. In Chapter 1 through Chapter 11, certain terms are in bold and italicized print. These terms appear again in the appendix, where more detailed information is provided.

The organization of this book is intended to enable you and/or your students to select the level of detailed planning assistance needed. The following are some examples.

- If student teachers wish to review the basics of lesson planning, the information in Chapters 5-10 will help remind them of what they already know.

- If student teachers demonstrate weaknesses in certain areas — e.g., planning lesson openings — supervisors may recommend the more detailed information available in the appendix.

- If student teachers or practicum students need support in writing plans, they can look at the sample plans in Chapters 4, 7, 8, 9, and 10.

- If practicum students are practicing certain

models or methods of teaching, they can select only those specific chapters or sections.

- If practicum students are attempting to plan lessons and activities and have not yet taken courses which teach certain methods — e.g., using peers — they can select those sections of chapters or look in the appendix for help.

- If instructors are using the text as a supplement to readings and instruction in courses, they can use sections as summaries or guides to completing practice assignments.

ACKNOWLEDGMENTS

Earlier drafts of this book were field tested with both practicum students and student teachers in special education and general education. All wrote lesson and activity plans using this book as a guide. As a result, many of them provided practical suggestions on the organization and content of the book. We are very grateful for their comments.

Valuable feedback also came from public school teachers and university instructors in both general and special education. We recognize and appreciate their gifts of time and ideas.

We would also like to acknowledge our extremely supportive families. They have provided us with encouragement during all phases of our project. Many, many thanks to Walter, Steve, Jerell, and Leah.

We owe a special thanks to Lyn Dyson, our friend and colleague. She very willingly read our manuscript countless times. She offered her support and so many valuable suggestions.

Daily Planning for Today's Classroom

Chapter 1

Introduction

PURPOSE

The purpose of this book is to help you learn how to teach so that all of your students will learn. You will learn to write detailed plans for activities and lessons which reflect each step of the thinking process needed for making good decisions for effective teaching. (This is analogous to teachers asking students to "show their work" when they are learning to solve math problems.) As you gain experience in planning, you will not need to write down as much detail. You will automatically think through the important components of planning, and you will make professional judgments about what to include and what to exclude in your lessons and activities.

The material in this book will not teach you to make curricular decisions. When you become a teacher, your responsibility will be to figure out *what* your students need to learn — the goals and objectives of the curriculum — and then *how* to teach them most effectively — the instruction needed. However, in your role as a practicum student or student teacher, you are being directed by a supervising teacher who has already made curricular decisions. Therefore, your primary responsibility will be to make instructional decisions.

When your cooperating teacher selects teaching opportunities for you, she/he may say any of the following:

▸ "Tomorrow I want you to do the morning opening" or "I'd like you to do the art activity next Tuesday. You may do anything you're interested in." When this happens, the teacher is asking you to plan an *activity* which may be scheduled on a daily, weekly, or monthly basis.

▸ "I want you to teach the children to make change" or "I want you to teach the difference between metaphors and similes." Here, the teacher is asking you to instruct students on a specific skill and/or to teach specific information; i.e., to teach a *lesson*.

▸ "I want you to teach about bats" or "I'd like you to teach Northwest Indian culture." In these examples, the teacher is assigning you a content topic to teach which could be done through either a lesson *or* an activity.

In each of these cases, you are going to write a plan. The type and components of the plan will vary, however, depending on the focus of what you will be teaching or implementing. That is what this book is all about — first, how to figure out what type of plan is needed and, then, what components need to be included in lesson and activity plans.

You are entering the teaching profession at a time when planning for a diverse group of students is not only a desirable skill for new teachers, but an essential one. Strategies for diversity will be addressed in Chapter 6; however, first it is necessary to find out about the students for whom you will be planning. It is important that you understand why such diversity exists in today's classrooms and why you are responsible for addressing it — whether you plan to be a special education teacher or a general education teacher.

THE REALITY OF DIVERSITY

It is commonly recognized that the student population in schools today is becoming increasingly diverse. This has a major impact on general education teachers. They must address the needs of students with diverse linguistic and cultural backgrounds. They are, additionally, being asked to teach students with disabilities. In years past, those students would have been served in programs outside the general education classroom or may not have been in school at all.

There have been lively discussions, as well as heated debates, about the diversity that exists in schools today. General education teachers are required to address a number of issues. First, they have had to rethink and revise what they teach and how they teach. They have also had to struggle with ambiguous feelings about ownership as students who present very significant challenges are placed in their classrooms. The general education teacher has had to establish a personal sense of responsibility for the school success of these students. Teaching *really is* more complex today, and teachers are struggling to effectively serve a growing diverse student population.

The Students

There are three major groups of students who contribute significantly to the diversity within classrooms today. Those are students with varied cultural and/or linguistic backgrounds; students considered "at risk;" and students with disabilities. They are all entering general education classrooms in growing numbers, and their presence has given new meaning to the term "general" education.

First, students with diverse cultural and linguistic backgrounds make up one group of students that has enriched the classroom of today. Their presence has created opportunities to learn about customs, beliefs, and traditions that may be outside the personal experiences of the teachers and other students. Many of those students, however, experience "culture shock" in classrooms where

their personal preferences for learning and performing do not match the expectations of their school setting. Making a successful transition to school can be extremely challenging for students who do not speak English. (It is not unusual to find several different languages spoken as primary languages by different students within one classroom.) Today's teacher must learn about individual student preferences and must find ways to honor and accommodate them. They may also need to help their students learn English. This teacher finds special challenges in helping the whole class of students respect and value the richness of their classmates' cultural variations (Garcia, 1994).

A second group of students coming to school in growing numbers is "at risk" for school failure. The factors that put these students at risk can be found both within our society at large and within our schools. The increase in drug and alcohol use/abuse, poverty, teen pregnancy, physical and emotional abuse, homelessness, and lack of supervision are only some of the societal problems that can cause students to come to school unprepared to learn. Factors at school can cause at risk behavior as well. Failure to recognize and/or address student learning problems, irrelevant curriculum, and poor teaching can significantly interfere with student progress. It is important to recognize that, while students at risk have problems that potentially interfere with success in school, many will not qualify for special education services or other special programs. These "unqualified" students depend exclusively on the general education teacher to meet their needs.

A third group of students that has contributed significantly to the diversity of the general education classroom is students with disabilities. When PL 94-142 (The Education for All Handicapped Children Act) was passed in 1975, it revolutionized service delivery to these students. The least restrictive environment (LRE) mandate in PL 94-142 was the first time in the history of special education that integration of students with disabilities was made a priority within all school

2

districts across the country. Placement in the LRE for students with disabilities often means spending time in the general education classroom. Today, the majority of these students remain in the general education classroom for at least part of their school day. Therefore, it is not unusual for a general education teacher to provide at least some services to several students with Individualized Education Programs (Hallahan & Kauffman, 1994).

Diversity in the schools is a reality. "Do you have any students with special needs in your classroom?" is no longer a relevant question to ask general education teachers. A much more appropriate one is, "How do you address the multitude of needs displayed by the students in your classroom?" The typical general education teacher today serves a wide range of students who pose significant challenges.

Your Responsibility

Your ability to be successful in working with a diverse student population begins with a feeling of responsibility to do so. If you believe that your job is to teach ALL students, then you will start off much better equipped to meet the challenge. If you believe that your job is to teach only those students who are easy to teach, then your ability to be effective is questionable. You will definitely spend a great deal of your time lamenting reality.

General education teachers today understandably struggle with the issues of diversity and responsibility. You may find yourself involved in discussions around the question, "Who is responsible for teaching the 'difficult to teach' student?" Insight into this question can be gained by examining the public school setup before and after special education legislation.

Years ago, prior to schools having separate special education teachers and classrooms, there was only one teacher for all students. Consequently, individual teachers felt a responsibility for teaching students who may have varied widely in age,

ability, and behavior. When challenged by a student who was especially difficult to teach, the teacher drew on her/his resourcefulness and experience. She/he tried all of the learned strategies and thought up new ones; e.g., adjusted presentations, materials, and activities; arranged for older students to tutor younger ones; organized students to work together on projects and activities; etc. These efforts were a response to the teacher's belief that it was her/his responsibility to teach all students. (*Note*: We recognize that until the 1970s schools were allowed to exclude students with significant physical, cognitive, and/or behavioral disabilities. The general education teacher's responsibility was typically to students with less severe disabilities and/or risk factors.)

The onset of special education as a separate entity had a major impact on the general classroom teacher's role in serving a diverse population of students. Students began being "sorted" according to whether or not they qualified for special education. If students did not qualify, they stayed in the general education classroom and were the responsibility of the general education teacher. When students did qualify for special education, they literally "moved out" of general education and "moved in" to special education, becoming the responsibility of the special education teacher. The idea of a shared responsibility for "difficult to teach" students did not exist.

The student "sorting" that occurred with the arrival of special education influenced the way general education teachers assumed responsibility toward students who posed significant challenges. It became common practice to send "problem students" out of the general education classroom so they could work with and be taught by specially trained teachers. The students who remained in the general education classroom were more similar in need and, frankly, easier to teach. Understandably, general classroom teachers no longer felt responsible for teaching students with significant needs because they *were* no longer responsible. An unfortunate side effect of the responsibility issue is that general education teachers lost confidence in their ability to serve these students.

The general education teacher is significantly influenced by special education reform. Today, this teacher is asked to accept responsibility for, and learn ways of, teaching students with disabilities. Inservice training professionals, teacher teams, and special education consultants all focus, at least in part, on helping teachers adjust. This adjustment includes developing self confidence and acquiring a belief that they can make a difference in the lives of all students. One can certainly appreciate the struggle of any teacher who wrestles with the issue of responsibility for serving students who are "difficult to teach."

PLANNING FOR DIVERSITY

The diversity in classrooms today requires a special kind of teacher. Regardless of the age and experience level of the teacher, this educator always views teaching as an important and exciting profession. This teacher feels a responsibility to teach all students and sees diversity as a fascinating challenge. Planning is done with the needs of all students in mind. She/he asks, "What strategies or methods can I incorporate into my lessons and activities that are most likely to ensure that ALL of my students will learn?" rather than "Now that I have my lesson prepared, I wonder if I have to change it for some of my students?" This teacher has a strong desire to learn, and she/he stays current in the field through reading professional journals and taking courses and workshops. This teacher develops an ever growing repertoire of teaching strategies and methods to use with challenging students. This teacher believes she/he can be effective and, therefore, is very effective in a diverse classroom. We hope you will become this teacher.

Lessons and activities must be planned with the needs of individual students as well as the needs of the whole group in mind. Many strategies that are essential for the success of students at risk or

students with disabilities may also be helpful to all students in the general education classroom. Information about specific strategies which are effective with a diverse group of students will be presented later in this text.

THE CONTENT AND ORGANIZATION OF THIS BOOK

This text provides information about the various components of the planning process, and it is organized to provide various levels of planning assistance. This makes it a versatile resource that can be utilized in your methods courses as well as practica, student teaching, and beyond.

Many aspects of planning are addressed in the pages that follow. Chapter 2 will help you decide which type of plan to write. Chapters 4, 5, and 7–10 will provide specific information about how to write activity and/or lesson plans. The sample activity plans and lesson plans located at the ends of Chapters 4 and 7–10 may help you better understand one or more of the planning components. Chapter 3 will furnish help with writing objectives. Chapter 6 includes many ideas for making your plans appropriate for the diverse student population which you will encounter in the schools. Finally, Chapter 11 will help you plan for effectively using the assistance of peers in your lessons and activities.

The organizational structure of this text is intended to enable you to select the specific content and the level of detail in planning assistance that you need. For example:

▸ If you want to review the basics of lesson planning, you can read the information in Chapters 5–10.

▸ If you are having specific problems during your student teaching experience — e.g., planning lesson openings — you may benefit from the more detailed information available in the appendix.

- If you are a practicum student practicing certain models or methods of teaching, you can select only the appropriate chapters or sections.

In most chapters some terms are bolded and italicized. These terms will appear again in the appendix where definitions or more detailed information are provided.

* *

REFERENCES

Brantlinger, E. "Influence of Preservice Teachers' Beliefs about Pupil Achievement on Attitudes Toward Inclusion." *Teacher Education and Special Education, 19.* pp. 17-33. 1996.

Garcia, E. *Understanding and Meeting the Challenge of Student Cultural Diversity.* Boston: Houghton Mifflin Company, 1994.

Hallahan, D., and J. Kauffman. *Exceptional Children.* 6th ed. Boston: Allyn and Bacon, 1994.

Levine, D.U., and F. Rayna. *Society and Education.* 9th ed. Boston: Allyn and Bacon, 1996.

Welch, M. "Teacher Education and the Neglected Diversity: Preparing Educators to Teach Students with Disabilities." *Journal of Teacher Education, 47.* pp. 355-366. 1996.

Chapter 2

Lessons and Activities — Which is Which?

INTRODUCTION

There are two reasons for distinguishing between lessons and activities. One is that each requires somewhat different planning decisions and tasks. The other is that, in our observations of practicum students and student teachers, when there is no clear distinction, we have noticed a common problem — forgetting to teach!

It is often difficult to clearly distinguish between lessons and activities because lessons typically include various activities. Additionally, because lessons vary in length — a lesson might last thirty minutes or three days — it can be difficult to determine when a lesson begins and when it ends; therefore, it is hard to know where an activity "fits." However, our objective is *not* that preservice teachers will be 100% accurate in telling apart lessons and activities. Our belief is that being aware of the differences between the two will help preservice teachers make good teaching decisions.

PRIMARY DIFFERENCES BETWEEN LESSONS AND ACTIVITIES

There are several ways in which lessons are different from activities. One way to distinguish between the two is to look at their *purposes*. The purpose of a lesson is to provide initial instruction on important skills or knowledge. Activities, on the other hand, may have a variety of purposes — learner motivation, additional experience, elaboration of information, additional practice, or integration or generalization of skills and knowledge.

Another way to distinguish between lessons and activities is to look at their *objectives*. A lesson has a specific, measurable, short-term objective, and the teacher's intention is that each student will meet that objective by the end of the lesson. Activities, typically, are used along with lessons to help students make progress toward long-term objectives or goals.

Because of the differences in objectives, the type of *evaluation* needed for lessons and activities differs. Lessons are followed by a formal evaluation of whether each student can independently meet the objective. The evaluations used with activities are often less formal and less individual.

The following sections provide further information and examples to help clarify the key differences between, and elements of, lessons and activities.

LESSONS

Lesson Example

In this lesson, you want to teach students to spell the plural form of nouns ending in y. The objective is that students will write the plural form of ten listed nouns ending in "y" preceded by a consonant; e.g., berry to berries. You instruct the students by explaining the spelling rule, showing examples, providing practice, and giving feedback. Another option would be to begin by showing examples and then leading the students to discover the spelling rule or pattern. Following the lesson, you evaluate by giving a test as described in the objective. (See Chapter 9 for a complete lesson plan for this objective.)

This is a lesson because you are providing *initial instruction* on an *important basic skill*; you are spending time *teaching*; and you intend to *evaluate* each student to see if they have met the *short-term objective following* the lesson.

Definition of Terms

The italicized terms in the above paragraph are defined as follows:

- **initial instruction**: "Initial" *does not* mean that students have never heard of the topic of the lesson before. They will typically have had some previous introduction, and the teacher will use strategies in the lesson to connect the new learning to prior knowledge and experience. If the students do not have the necessary background, then the teacher has selected the wrong objective/lesson to teach at this time. "Initial" *does* mean that the students need formal instruction before they can use the new knowledge or skill. They need more than review and practice.

- **important basic skill**: Important basic skills include academic skills, thinking skills, study skills, social skills, vocational skills, etc. They are considered basic because they are either important for "real life" functioning or they are necessary prerequisites for other important skills. (One could make a case that the skill in the above spelling lesson example is not important in an age of computers with spell check capabilities.)

- **teaching**: Teaching can take many forms. It can be highly teacher directed; it can incorporate peers; it can emphasize discovery. However, teaching means that the teacher does more than provide activities, hoping that students learn something. If no teaching is necessary, you do not have a lesson. Instead, you have either an activity or a "time filler."

- **evaluate**: When you write the lesson objective, you establish a standard against which you intend to evaluate *each* student's learning and you decide how you are going to evaluate it. There are many ways to evaluate — not only written tests. If you do not want to evaluate, you are probably not providing initial instruction on an important basic skill; i.e., you do not have a lesson. If your intention is to provide an "experience," you may have an activity, not a lesson. If your intention is to ask students to demonstrate their knowledge or skill with the help of peers or teacher, you have an ongoing practice activity, not a completed lesson.

- **short-term objective**: Lessons are intended to help students reach a measurable short-term objective. A series of lessons, often combined with activities, leads to the attainment of long-term objectives/goals.

Long and short are relative terms. We cannot give exact definitions or numbers but consider this example. Mrs. Lopez wants her students to learn to add and subtract fractions with unlike denominators. She breaks that long-term objective or goal into several short-term objectives such as finding least common multiples, converting improper fractions, etc. She will plan a lesson for each of those short-term objectives. Mrs. Lopez may decide to teach the lesson on least common multiples in twenty minute periods over three days. She considers this one lesson because she is not going to formally evaluate until after the third day. But she will want to evaluate each students' success with finding least common multiples before going on to the next lesson.

The students will not have received all of the necessary instruction to reach the short-term objective until day three.

- **following**: To evaluate the objective following the lesson may mean immediately after the lesson or may mean one day or several days after the lesson. You may need to provide extended practice before evaluating, or you may have found, through monitoring, that you need to reteach before evaluating. However, if you do not intend to evaluate for weeks or months, you are planning to evaluate whether students meet a long-term objective/goal, not a short-term lesson objective.

Summary

You begin planning a lesson by selecting a specific, measurable, short-term objective. Then you provide opportunities to learn. You follow the lesson with an evaluation to determine whether each student can independently meet the objective.

ACTIVITIES

Activities are not intended to provide initial instruction and do not include the same evaluation as lessons. Activities may lead up to lessons, be part of lessons, follow up lessons, or extend lessons. Activities have a variety of *purposes*. Some are the following:

- to motivate students before beginning a series of lessons

- to provide background information or experience and to recall prior knowledge before a series of lessons. (*Note*: A lesson typically includes an opening with strategies to motivate students or to help them connect this lesson with prior knowledge. We are differentiating this from longer, more elaborate activities used before a series of lessons.)

- to provide ongoing practice toward long-term objectives/goals.

- to provide opportunities for students to apply/generalize a previously learned skill.

- to provide opportunities for students to integrate a variety of skills learned in lessons in different subject areas.

Although activities are not associated with a specific short-term objective, they are planned with a definite intention. Teachers develop activities as part of their long-term planning and have a clear purpose for activities which help their students reach important goals and objectives. Teachers also use activities to help evaluate student needs and progress. Even though activities are not always paired with formal evaluations of individuals, teachers carefully observe their students during activities and/or examine the products that students create in order to make decisions about the need for additional activities and lessons.

Activity Examples

The following examples illustrate the wide variety of activity purposes:

- Before beginning a series of lessons on magnets, you plan an *activity* in which you give students different types of magnets and materials and have them experiment, make predictions, generate questions, etc. Your purposes are to create interest and to motivate the students to learn more about magnets; to make sure each student has experience with magnets before beginning the lessons; and to provide practice on thinking skills. You also use this activity to assess prior knowledge to help you decide where to begin your lessons.

- Every day Mrs. Chenier writes a sentence that is full of errors on the blackboard. Students are to copy the sentence and fix the errors. This is an *activity* to provide ongoing practice on proofreading for errors in capitalization, punctuation, spelling, etc. — not to give initial instruction on written mechanics.

▸ Students have had earlier lessons on how to write letters. You now plan an *activity* in which students write letters to the agricultural extension agent asking for information on rabbit care. (There is a pet rabbit in the classroom.) You may choose to review earlier lessons at the beginning of the activity, but you are not providing initial instruction on letter writing.

▸ Students are making a garden in the school yard. They use measuring skills learned in math; use information about plant needs for light and water learned in science; and use group decision-making skills learned in social skills lessons in order to select the vegetables to be planted. This is an *activity* intended to help students integrate and apply skills learned in a variety of subject areas.

▸ Following math lessons on the multiplication concept and operation, your students can figure out the answers to single digit multiplication problems, but they are not always 100% accurate and they are very slow. You plan a series of practice *activities* — partner flash card practice and multiplication bingo — to help the students reach your long-term objective. The objective is that students will write answers to multiplication fact problems (0-10) at a rate of 80 digits per minute with no errors. In this case you follow each activity with a timed math fact test in order to chart individual student progress toward the objective.

▸ The week before January 15th, Mr. Vandermay shows a video and leads a discussion about Dr. Martin Luther King, Jr. as the first in a series of *activities* leading up to Dr. King's birthday. His goal is to provide general information about a famous American and to make sure his students understand the upcoming holiday. He

has not written a short-term objective and plans no evaluation.

▸ Mr. Palm plans an *activity* in which he reads a story to his second graders about polar bears and then helps the students put together a book which includes drawings and sentences about polar bears. Mr. Palm is providing initial instruction, in a sense, since his students do not know many of the facts about polar bears discussed in the book. However, he does not really care whether each student memorizes these facts and does not intend to give a test on polar bears. Polar bears are a vehicle for providing ongoing practice on listening skills, fine motor skills, writing complete sentences, etc. As he looks at the students' books, he will monitor progress ("I see that Ralph is still forgetting to put a period at the end of his sentences."), but there is no short-term objective with a formal evaluation. Mr. Palm may have other goals as well — to pique curiosity about animals and nature or to give the students experience in being authors.

▸ Mrs. Eerkes plans an *activity* to follow a series of lessons on the Civil War. It will be a simulated debate in Congress on the issue of preserving the union versus states' rights. The students will be divided into two groups and given time to research the issues and to plan their speeches. She has several purposes for this activity: to provide practice in public speaking and cooperative planning and research; to encourage a deeper understanding of the issues involved; and to allow the students to demonstrate their knowledge in an alternative way. She knows that this activity will not allow her to be aware of each student's understanding independently, so she has planned other evaluation methods as well.

▸ An art *activity* is planned in which you will teach your students to tie-dye. You will include many of the elements of lesson planning — step by step instruction, demonstrations, and supervised practice. You consider this an

9

activity because tie-dyeing is not an important basic skill (anymore), and, because even though each student will produce a tie-dyed item, they will do so with your help. You are not planning to test them later, either by asking them to list the steps in tie-dyeing or by asking them to make a tie-dyed item alone.

Summary

Lessons have been defined very narrowly and activities have been defined very broadly. Lessons have a consistent structure and involve "hands-on teaching." Activities lack one or more of the attributes of a lesson and have many purposes and structures. Both need to be carefully planned.

SELECTING
THE APPROPRIATE PLAN

During a practicum or student teaching, the two basic types of plans that you will need to know how to write are the activity plan and the lesson plan. Both require careful thought and, with practice, become easier and less time consuming to write. As your understanding of important planning components increases, your decision making will become more automatic and fewer details will need to be put in writing.

When your cooperating teacher gives you a teaching assignment, you need to analyze the request carefully so that you will know whether you need to write an activity plan or a lesson plan. Ask yourself the following questions:

▸ Am I being asked to provide initial instruction?

▸ Am I being asked to teach an important basic skill?

▸ Can I write a specific, measurable, short-term objective for this topic?

▸ Will I need to spend time teaching (rather than only reviewing or giving directions)?

▸ Will I want to evaluate whether each student can independently meet the objective of the lesson?

♦ If your answer to ALL of these questions is "yes," then turn to Chapter 5 "Lesson Plans."

♦ If your answer to ANY of these questions is "no," then turn to Chapter 4 "Activity Plans."

Figure 2.1 provides a summary of the decisions that help you determine when to write a lesson plan and when to write an activity plan.

* * * * * * * * * * * * * * * * * * *

Figure 2.1 LESSON PLAN OR ACTIVITY PLAN?

ASK YOURSELF THE FOLLOWING QUESTIONS:
— Am I being asked to provide initial instruction?

— Am I being asked to teach an important basic skill?

— Will I spend time teaching?

— Can I write a specific, measurable, short-term objective for this topic?

— Will I want to evaluate whether each student can independently meet
the objective following the lesson?

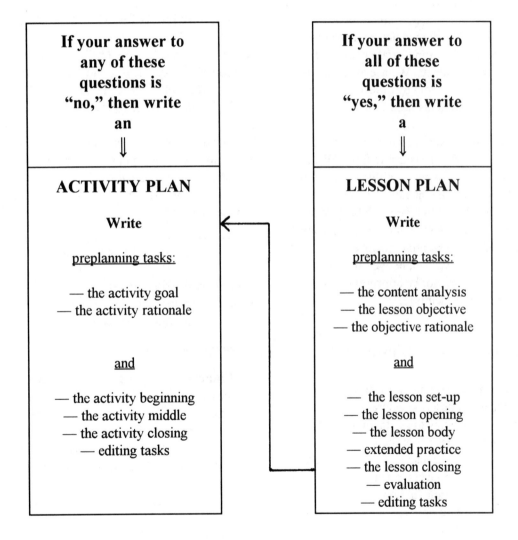

**If your answer to
any of these
questions is
"no," then write
an**

⇓

ACTIVITY PLAN

Write

<u>preplanning tasks:</u>

— the activity goal
— the activity rationale

<u>and</u>

— the activity beginning
— the activity middle
— the activity closing
— editing tasks

**If your answer to
all of these
questions is
"yes," then write
a**

⇓

LESSON PLAN

Write

<u>preplanning tasks:</u>

— the content analysis
— the lesson objective
— the objective rationale

<u>and</u>

— the lesson set-up
— the lesson opening
— the lesson body
— extended practice
— the lesson closing
— evaluation
— editing tasks

Chapter 3

Writing Objectives

INTRODUCTION

An effective activity or lesson plan begins with an appropriate, clearly written objective. However, as stated earlier, planning the curriculum is beyond the scope of this book. We are not going to teach you to select or develop appropriate goals and objectives for your students. We are assuming that you know, or have been told by your cooperating teacher, what your students need to learn next.

We are going to teach you a format for *writing* objectives in a specific, measurable form. Writing those objectives will make it more likely that your activity or lesson and the intended learning outcome will match and that you will be able to tell if your teaching was effective; i.e., whether your students learned. It is essential, however, to remember that objectives can be well written in terms of form and, yet, not be appropriate or important for your student(s).

DEFINITION AND PURPOSE

An objective is a description of a learning outcome. Objectives describe where we want students to go — not how to get them there. They pinpoint the destination — not the journey. Well written objectives help teachers clarify precisely what they want their students to learn; help provide lesson focus and direction; and help guide the selection of appropriate practice activities. They give teachers a way to evaluate whether or not their students have learned and therefore a way to measure their own teaching effectiveness. They also help focus and motivate students, and they are

a communication tool with other teachers and parents.

COMPONENTS OF OBJECTIVES

Well written, measurable objectives include four components: content, behavior, condition, and criterion (Howell, Fox, and Morehead, 1993, p. 42). Including these four components will help ensure that your objectives are clear and specific. Each of the four components is briefly described below and examples and nonexamples are provided. Common errors may be noted and suggestions for writing each objective component may be included.

☞ Example Objective

Students will write answers on a worksheet to twenty subtraction problems, two-digit numbers from three-digit numbers with regrouping, with no errors.

- **Content**: The content is the subject matter. It tells what the student will learn. In the objective above, the content is "subtraction problems, two-digit numbers from three-digit numbers with regrouping." Note that the content is described specifically so that anyone reading the objective understands what the student will learn.

- **Behavior**: The behavior tells what the student will do to show that she/he has learned. It is a verb which describes an observable action. In the objective above, the behavior is "write." The student will demonstrate knowledge of subtraction by writing the answers to problems.

- **Condition**: It is important to describe the conditions — circumstances, situation, or setting — under which the student will perform the behavior. It is the condition which will apply while the student is being evaluated, rather than the learning condition, which must be described. In the objective above, the condition is "on a worksheet."

- **Criterion**: The criterion is the level of acceptable performance, the standard of mastery, or the proficiency level expected. This component describes how well the student should perform in order to say that she/he has met the objective. In the objective above, the criterion is "with no errors."

Content

This component describes the specific subject matter to be learned.

<u>Suggestions When Writing the Content</u>

1. Be **specific** enough that anyone reading the objective will understand the subject matter.

2. Be sure the description of content can stand alone; i.e., be "**materials free**." The reader should be able to understand the content of the objective without tracking down specific materials.

3. Be **generic** enough that the emphasis is on knowledge and skills that are important and applicable in a variety of contexts.

☞ <u>Examples of Content</u>

▸ Add <u>unlike fractions with common factors between denominators</u>.

▸ Write <u>two syllable spelling words with -ing endings; e.g., hoping, hopping</u>.
▸ Compare and contrast <u>fables and fairy tales</u>.

⊠ <u>Nonexamples of Content</u>

▸ Add <u>fractions</u> (not specific); answer <u>fractions problems #1-7 on p. 42</u> (not "materials free").
▸ Write <u>spelling words</u> (not specific); complete <u>Unit 4 in spelling book</u> (not "materials free").
▸ Compare and contrast <u>"The Lazy Princess" and "Lost in the Woods"</u> (not generic).

<u>Common Error When Writing the Content</u>

A common error is to include content appropriate for an activity or assignment rather than a learning outcome. For example:

1. Write <u>adjectives for ten animals and plants from the rainforest unit.</u> Are you looking for knowledge of the rainforest or knowledge of adjectives? This may be a good integrated practice activity, but it is not a clear objective.

2. Present five <u>facts about a bird of their choice.</u> The content is unclear. We do not know what facts nor what bird. Is the "real" content using reference books to find facts; or making presentations; or summarizing from the unit on birds? Do not confuse an instructional theme with content.

Behavior

This component states what students will do to demonstrate their learning. The behavior or performance is written as an observable verb so that outcomes can be measured.

☞ <u>Examples of Behavior</u>
---

say	write	list
draw	diagram	paraphrase
operate	throw	volunteer
circle	complete	copy

label	predict	calculate
add	design	select
name	hit	laugh
choose	initiate	put in order
define	compare/contrast	

Notice that some of these verbs can be made more specific; e.g., one could "define" in writing or orally. You must judge how much specificity is needed, but when in doubt be more specific rather than less. For example, the commonly used verbs "identify" and "recognize" often need further specifics, such as "identify by underlining."

⊠ Nonexamples of Behavior

know	realize	comprehend
understand	experience	discover
memorize	believe	appreciate
learn	value	be familiar with

Notice that these verbs may be appropriate when writing *general* goals, aims, outcomes, or standards. They are not appropriate for measurable objectives because you cannot know that a student "knows" or "comprehends" or has "learned" something unless she/he does something overt. For example, you may have a goal that your students appreciate poetry. You cannot tell if that objective has been reached unless your students do something — voluntarily check out poetry books from the library or write poetry without being assigned to do so.

Suggestions When Writing the Behavior

1. Decide whether you want students to "identify" or "produce" as you write the behavior component in objectives (Howell, Fox, and Morehead, 1993, p. 42). A lesson for teaching students to *produce*/write metaphors will be quite different from a lesson for teaching students to *identify*/recognize metaphors written by someone else.

2. Include only one or two behaviors in an objective. Objectives which include many behaviors — i.e., student will research and write and draw and present... — make evaluation confusing and often end up being descriptions of activities or assignments rather than learning outcomes.

3. Leave out nonessential or redundant behaviors; for example:

    ▸ "Student will *copy* the sentences and *circle* all nouns..." Omit "copy the sentences." It has nothing to do with the skill of identifying nouns.

    ▸ "Student will *locate* and *point* to..." Omit "locate." If the student is pointing to something, then you can assume she/he has located it.

4. Omit the phrase "be able to" as in the example "The student will be able to make a speech..." The phrase adds words but no meaning. Remember that the performance is important, not an assumed ability or inability.

5. Do not use the phrase "Student will pass a test on..." It does not communicate specific information about what the student will do/learn.

6. Write objectives for what the student(s) will do, not what the teacher will do. Objectives may be written for one student or a group of students.

Conditions

Describing the evaluation condition(s) provides additional specificity about what the student will learn. Notice that the underlined conditions in the following objectives result in three different learning outcomes.

▸ Students will write the capitals of each of the 17 western states <u>given a list of the states and a list of the capitals</u>. (They will be asked to recognize state capitals. This is really a matching task.)

▸ Students will write the capitals of each of the 17 western states given a list of the states. (They will be asked to recall the state capitals rather than simply recognize them.)

▸ Students will write the capitals of each of the 17 western states on a blank outline map. (They must recall the names and locations of the states and the names of the capitals in order to write the capitals in the correct places.)

Notice that the different conditions affect the difficulty level of the objective and will affect the lesson and practice activities which you plan for your students.

Types of Conditions

There are various types of conditions which may be included in objectives. A very important condition is whether we are asking students to perform a skill *in isolation or in context* (Howell, Fox, and Morehead, 1993, p. 43) or in artificial or in real-world circumstances. This is important to think about when sequencing objectives and when planning for generalization or transfer of the skill. The *information or materials provided* — often called the "givens" — may be important to specify. Visualize the evaluation/testing situation and what the students will have available. A third type of condition — a description of the *setting or situation* — may help clarify the objective as well, especially social skill and learning strategy objectives. Obviously all conditions need not be mentioned; e.g., the lights will be on in the room. However, be sure to include those which communicate important information about the learning outcome.

═══════════════════════════════════
☞ Examples of Conditions
═══════════════════════════════════

▸ **In isolation or in context**

- computing measurement equivalents on a worksheet or while following a recipe
- responding to teasing in a role-play or on the playground
- correcting punctuation errors in given sentences or while proofreading an essay
- pronouncing words when shown flashcards or in a story

Note: You may want to specify whether the student is going to solve mixed math problems or correct mixed grammar errors. Otherwise, you may only be evaluating whether students can figure out the pattern; e.g., all problems require regrouping or all sentences are missing a question mark.

▸ **Information or materials provided**
- on a diagram
- given a list of ten nouns
- given a description of symptoms
- given an incomplete proof
- given population figures for each country
- with a calculator, ruler, scale
- using notes, dictionary, word processor
- from memory; i.e., nothing provided

▸ **Setting or situation**
- while presenting in front of class
- during seatwork; on homework
- in familiar situations; with strangers
- when given directions
- when corrected
- during class discussions
- during teacher presentations
- when working with a small group of peers
- during free time
- when given a choice
- on an in-class test
- in a textbook
- when teased; when angry; when refused

▸ Often a **combination of conditions** are specified
- given ten problems and a calculator

▸ In some cases — for example, when writing

objectives for students with severe disabilities or for very young students — it may be important to specify whether students will be performing the behavior **independently or with assistance.**

- with or without reminders
- with or without physical assistance
- with or without verbal cues

Note: Typically the "default" condition is without assistance.

⊠ Nonexamples of Conditions

▸ **Describing the learning condition rather than the evaluation condition.** It doesn't matter where or when the students learned the knowledge or skill. Remember that objectives focus on outcomes. Do *not* use:
  - as a result of my instruction
  - after a lesson on...
  - after completing the weather unit
  - after studying

▸ **Adding unimportant information.** Some conditions are obvious and do not need to be written. Do *not* use:
  - when asked by the teacher
  - given a blank piece of paper

Criterion

The criterion specifies the standard of acceptable performance. It states how well the student must perform in order to say that she/he has met the objective.

☞ Examples of Criterion

▸ **As a total number or proportion**
  - comparing/contrasting on four key issues
  - using two types of figurative language
  - at every opportunity
  - in three/three trials
  - at least five times daily
  - with no errors

- with ten/ten correct
- with 90% accuracy
- at least three of the steps
- five paragraphs in length

▸ **In terms of time**
  - within ten minutes; per minute
  - for one hour each day
  - the first time
  - for five consecutive days
  - by September 6

▸ **As a variation**
  - within plus or minus one inch
  - to the nearest mile
  - within one percent
  - to the closest hundredth

▸ **As a description or result**
  - light bulb turns on
  - liquid disappears
  - until consensus is reached
  - story includes a conflict and resolution
  - the strategy selected solves the problem in the fewest steps

▸ Often the criterion is a **combination** of the above
  - fifty per minute with 100% accuracy by March 10
  - backing up opinion with data from three relevant research studies
  - paragraphs include topic sentences and at least three supporting details

⊠ Nonexamples of Criterion

▸ **Does not pass the "stranger test"**
  - as judged by teacher
  - to teacher's satisfaction

These obviously do not pass the "stranger test" (Kaplan, 1995, p. 56); i.e., they are open to interpretation. A stranger may not interpret them the same way as you do. Remember that one of the purposes of writing objectives is to communicate

16

clearly with students, parents, and other teachers and professionals.

Common Errors When Writing the Criterion

1. **The criterion is too low.** Keep high performance standards, especially for basic skills in reading, writing, and arithmetic. Do not confuse setting criteria in objectives with assigning grades. It will take some students longer to reach an objective. You may want to set gradually increasing criteria — 50% accuracy by October 1; 75% accuracy by November 1; 100% accuracy by December 1. However, be sure that the final outcome is high enough. If a student is only 80% accurate on number recognition, she/he is doomed to failure in arithmetic.

2. **The criterion is set arbitrarily.** Do not make the error of automatically writing 85% accuracy for every objective. Set realistic standards and time limits. Establish criteria either by doing the task yourself or by having a successful peer do the task. DO NOT WRITE: "...will say the multiples of 10 from 10 to 100 in three minutes" or "...locates a word in the dictionary in five minutes." Try it! If it took you five minutes to find a word, you would never choose to use the dictionary.

3. **"Percent accuracy" is misused.**

   ▸ When there are many possible divergent or complex responses, percent accuracy as the criterion does not make sense. One cannot write a story with 100% accuracy nor manage anger with 80% accuracy.

   ▸ There needs to be a number of responses for percent accuracy to be sensible — not simply correct or incorrect. For example, choose "name the state you live in" or "correctly name the state you live in" rather than "name the state you live in with 100% (50%?) accuracy." Write "turn off the computer correctly, or without

damaging anything" rather than "turn off the computer with 100% accuracy."

   ▸ Sometimes percent accuracy works, but it would be too much work to compute. To decide if someone reached 85% accuracy in punctuating a story, you would first have to count all of the opportunities for punctuation within the story.

4. **There is no end in sight.** If the objective is that the student will spell words correctly in all
written work, when would you be able to say that a student had met this objective?

Suggestions When Writing the Criterion

1. Think about how many times you want the students to demonstrate the skill during evaluation in order to be confident that they have met the objective. For example, do they need to write their addresses five times to prove they can do it? If Jon responds to teasing appropriately during one recess, are you sure he has learned that skill?

2. Be specific enough so that any evaluator would reach the same conclusion as to whether the student meets the objective.

   NOT SPECIFIC: "Student will write **descriptive** sentences." This criterion is not specific enough to evaluate the following two samples in order to determine if the objective of the lesson has been met: "The bike is big." "Perched on the seat of the bike, I felt like Hillary on the peak of Everest."

3. Make sure the criterion gets at the skill you want. For example, if the skill you are looking for is writing descriptively, do not make your criterion say that all words need to be spelled correctly. In addition, do not write a criterion solely because it is easy to think of; e.g., "Student will underline the adjectives in a given sentence without error."

Note: In attempting to make the objective specific and measurable, do not end up making it trivial!

SUMMARY

1. Write objectives which describe learning *outcomes*, not activities or assignments (TenBrink, 1994, p. 58).

   NOT: Wally will write spelling words missed on the pretest five times each.

   NOT: Students in pairs will take turns throwing dice, adding the numbers together, and stating the total.

   NOT: Students will play a quiz show game in which they divide into two teams and answer questions from Chapter 4 in the social studies book. Each team will ask questions to the other side.

   NOT: Ben will write letters to the main character in the story.

2. Keep objectives clean and simple; save creativity for instruction.

   NOT: Students will demonstrate their understanding of the reasons that bald eagles were endangered by graphing the average number of eagle babies born and the number of eagles who died per year for the last ten years.

   NOT: Students will create a poster which demonstrates their knowledge of modern Mexican culture.

3. Be sure to write objectives which represent *important* learning outcomes!

   NOT: Michelle will write the names of the counties in each state in the United States from memory without error.

☞ <u>Examples of Measurable Objectives</u>

▶ Given ten sets of five pictures, four of which are related — belong to the same category, such as vegetables or tools — students will point to the one in each set which does not belong, without error.

▶ Students will correctly state temperatures, with an accuracy of + or - 1 degree, shown on pictures of five thermometers depicting temperatures between -20 degrees F. and 95 degrees F.

▶ Randi will write correct answers to five/five inference questions on a grade level reading passage.

▶ Students will return the change from $1.00, using the fewest possible coins, for four purchases, with no errors.

▶ When the fire alarm sounds for a fire drill, students will form a line within thirty seconds and leave the building following the correct route, without teacher prompting.

▶ Kathi and Chuck will correctly compute the amount of wallpaper needed to cover a wall of given dimensions.

▶ When teased by peers, Jorge will respond by ignoring, walking away, or quietly asking the person to stop in eight out of eight observed opportunities by May 1.

▶ Richard Michael will complete all of his independent seatwork assignments during class with at least 90% accuracy for two consecutive weeks.

A Final Thought

We wish to restate the importance of beginning your lesson or activity planning with a clear idea of what you want your students to learn. Writing a specific objective will cause you to think this through. It has been our experience that, when a preservice teacher experiences frustration with a particular lesson or activity, it is often the case that she/he is unable to clearly state what students were to learn. Writing a clear objective is well worth your time.

* *

STUDY SUGGESTIONS
PRACTICING WRITING OBJECTIVES

Once you have mastered the skill of writing clear objectives, planning useful activities and lessons will be easier and less time consuming. Following are strategies to help you become accurate and fluent at writing objectives. As with other writing tasks, editing and rewriting will always be important.

1. Study the component names and definitions. Paraphrase them.

2. Review the lists of component examples. Explain why each example fits the definition. Create your own examples.

3. Practice writing your own objectives.

    a. Think of a general instructional goal, such as:
        -   knows how to use an index
        -   learns baseball skills
        -   understands cell division
        -   distinguishes between fact and fiction
        -   resolves conflicts nonviolently
        -   does homework

    b. Specify the content; e.g., index → subject index in textbook.

    c. Specify the behavior; e.g., knows how to use → locates page numbers for topics.

    d. Add necessary conditions; e.g., given a textbook and a list of topics.

    e. Add criteria; e.g., no errors, within thirty seconds.

        Note: Notice that there are many possibilities for each component. You may wish to practice writing a variety of objectives on one topic.

    f. Put the components together into a one or two sentence objective.

        Example: Given a textbook and a list of topics, the student will locate page numbers for topics in the subject index in the textbook with no errors, within thirty seconds.

g. Examine for clarity and conciseness and rewrite as necessary.

Example: Given a textbook, the student will write the correct page number from the index for four/four listed topics within two minutes.

4. After you have written an objective, critique it following these self-evaluation steps:

a. Are all four components present? (Label them.)

b. Is each component correct?
- content specific? generic? materials free?
- behavior observable?
- *evaluation* condition described?
- criterion specific? measurable? realistic?

c. Does the objective need editing? Is it wordy? Is it awkward?

d. Does it pass the stranger test?

e. Does it represent an important learning outcome?

REFERENCES

Howell, K.W., S.L. Fox, and M.K. Morehead. *Curriculum-Based Evaluation: Teaching and Decision Making.* 2nd ed. Pacific Grove, CA: Brooks/Cole, 1993.

Kaplan, J.S. *Beyond Behavior Modification.* 3rd ed. Austin, TX: Pro-Ed, 1995.

TenBrink, T.D. "Instructional Objectives." In J.M. Cooper (Ed.) *Classroom Teaching Skills.* 5th ed. pp. 55-84. Lexington, MA: D.C. Heath, 1994.

Chapter 4

Activity Plans

INTRODUCTION

Teachers typically use a wide variety of activities during the school day. Some of these activities are necessary routines to organize and manage all of the things that need to be done, such as correcting homework or getting ready to go home. Others are meant as fun or relaxing activities to provide a break for students, such as listening to music or singing a song. Certain activities occur daily; e.g., math timings. Others may happen only occasionally; e.g., watching a fun video. This chapter is *not* about how to plan the above types of activities except in those cases where the activity is quite complex; e.g., morning opening activities. (See Sample Activity Plan #3 which appears at the end of this chapter.)

This chapter *is* about how to plan for activities which are directly related to the curriculum — activities which extend, supplement, and/or enrich lessons. The purpose or rationale for any given activity may not be immediately apparent to an observer, but it is very clear to the teacher. As discussed in Chapter 2, teachers use activities which relate to the regular curriculum with various purposes in mind.

Purposes of Activities

▸ to *motivate* students before or during a series of lessons; e.g., planning class fund-raising activities before beginning a unit on economics.

▸ to provide *background information* or to enrich students' knowledge and experience before or during a series of lessons; e.g., taking a field trip to a salmon hatchery while studying resource conservation.

▸ to provide *ongoing practice* toward long-term objectives; e.g., playing math games to increase fluency on addition facts or doing art activities which provide practice using fine motor skills or following directions.

▸ to provide opportunities for students to *apply or generalize* a previously learned skill; e.g., having students plan and maintain a daily meal and snack plan which meets basic food group requirements.

▸ to provide opportunities for students to *integrate* a variety of skills learned in lessons in different subject areas; e.g., having students write letters to the editor of the local newspaper about pertinent social issues being discussed in social studies in order to practice their writing skills.

IMPORTANT: As you will see in Chapter 5, the various components of a *lesson plan* may have the same purposes noted above for activities; e.g., the opening of a lesson may be intended to motivate students. In addition, lessons always include practice activities (see supervised and extended practice components), and they sometimes incorporate activities to supplement the presentation of information component. For example, the teacher may show a video tape about the main parts of the heart and their functions during a lesson on the circulatory system. When activities are part of a daily lesson, the planning for their implementation is written into the lesson plan itself. When activities are part of a *series* of lessons or unit or when activities are long and complex, then writing a separate activity plan will be helpful.

The teacher typically decides what activities will be used while doing long-term or unit planning. The teacher may also plan additional activities based on his/her assessment of student progress. For example, the teacher may find that students need more practice on identifying adjectives than originally planned.

GENERIC COMPONENTS OF AN ACTIVITY PLAN

An activity plan is a written description of exactly what the teacher will do and say to help students prepare for and complete an activity. It may consist of some or all of the following: a set of questions to ask; explanations which help tie the current activity to other learning; step-by-step directions.

All activity plans contain the same generic components even though the content of each component will vary greatly, depending on the type of activity being planned. For example, a plan for showing and discussing a video tape will look very different from a plan written for a complex art project. The following explains the purpose of each component and suggests the kinds of decisions that need to be made in each. This is designed to help guide you through the steps for planning your activity. When you are ready to actually write an activity plan, refer to Figure 4.1 "Writing An Activity Plan."

Component 1 - Preplanning Tasks

The first task is deciding what you wish to accomplish — e.g., to motivate students, to provide opportunities for integrating skills, to provide practice toward a long term objective, and to write the *activity goal* and *activity rationale*.

Do not make the mistake of selecting an activity first and then trying to justify it by making up a goal and rationale (see appendix).

Once you have decided on the goal, then brainstorm activities which will bring about this goal or outcome. Be creative. Consider variety, novelty, and student interests. Think about the diversity in your classroom and what kinds of activities would be flexible enough to provide opportunities for all students to be challenged and successful. Select the activity which best fits the goal and the students.

Note: If you are a practicum student or student teacher, your cooperating teacher may already have decided on the goal and the type of activity. For example, she/he may ask you to plan an art activity which will fit with the unit on Northwest Native Americans or to find a book to read to the students which introduces the theme of friendship.

Component 2 - Activity Beginning

The purpose of the activity beginning is to prepare the students for the start of the activity and for participating and learning. You will need to decide on a signal for gaining the students' attention, as well as methods of regaining attention during the activity. If the activity will involve a lot of noise or involve a lot of student movement, you will probably want to use a strong *signal for attention* — such as ringing a bell or flicking the lights.

It is also necessary to think about your expectations for student behavior during the activity and how you will explain them to the students. For example, may they draw while listening to the story? Are there special rules for using the materials? May they ask for help from peers? Stating your expectations directly is an important strategy for preventing behavior problems. Plan what you will say and when you will say it. Write your *statement of behavior expectations*.

It is very important that you think about how you will help students understand the purpose of the activity and how it connects with lessons and with their prior knowledge and personal experience. You will want to capture their interest right away and motivate them to participate. Write your plan for the *opening*.

Component 3 - Activity Middle

The activity middle is a specific description of what the students and the teacher will do during the activity. This will be the most detailed and longest section of the plan and must be thought through carefully.

The planning decisions in this section will be very different depending on the type of activity being planned. However, there are certain planning elements which should always be considered because they will help meet the diverse needs of the students. One key element is to provide information both verbally and visually. For example, write the rules for a game on a poster as well as saying them to the students, or demonstrate the preparation of a microscope slide as well as providing a list of procedures. Another key element is to incorporate *active participation* by all students during the activity. For example, when asking questions during a story, have students say their response to a neighbor rather than calling on only one or two volunteers. A third element is to plan provisions which take into account individual strengths and weaknesses. These might include allowing options, such as (a) having students work individually, or with partners, or in small groups, or (b) asking students to make a presentation rather than writing a report. (See Chapters 6 and 11 for many additional ideas.)

Remember to:

▸ provide information both verbally and visually.
▸ incorporate active participation.
▸ plan provisions for individual differences.

Think about your activity — what you will be doing; what the students will be doing; and what you will need to communicate to your students. If the students will be listening to or watching something (e.g., readings, films, demonstrations), you will need to plan a set of questions to ask or a series of explanations to make. If the students will be creating something (e.g., writing, drawing, building), you will need to plan a set of directions to give and perhaps plan to show an example of a finished product. If the students are going to be doing something (e.g., performing experiments or playing a game), you will need to plan a set of procedures or rules.

You May Need to Plan:

▸ *a set of questions* — questions you plan to ask before, during, and after reading a story, playing a musical selection, or taking students on a nature walk. It can be difficult to ask good questions spontaneously. Planning some of the questions in advance will help you ask clear and thought provoking ones. It will also help you think through the purposes of the questions — recalling details, predicting, summarizing. Be sure to plan how you will ask for responses as well.

▸ *a series of statements or explanations* — explaining to students that the video tape they are about to see presents three major factors that contribute to child abuse and that, when the video is over, they need to be prepared to discuss them. Telling students what to watch or listen for will help them focus. Planning these statements in advance will ensure clarity and brevity.

▸ *a list of directions* — the step by step directions for the book covers students will be making for the short stories they have written. Displaying the directions in writing, as well as stating the directions to the students, is very important and will save much repetition.

23

Planning the directions in advance will ensure clarity and completeness.

- *a sample of a finished product* — an example of a completed book cover. Seeing a completed product can be very helpful in understanding what to do and what is expected. Be sure to clarify whether students' products need to look exactly like the sample or whether you are looking for variety and creativity. If the steps in making the product are complex, consider showing samples of the product at various stages of completion.

- *a list of procedures* — procedures for how to experiment with each magnet; how to find partners or form groups; how to share tasks; where to get or how to use materials or equipment, etc. In addition to stating the procedures, showing the written list or even acting them out is helpful.

- *a list of rules* — the rules for the quiz show game the students will be playing to review social studies information prior to their test. Again, providing a written summary of the rules as well as stating them is a good idea. Be sure to plan all needed rules in order to avoid confusion, arguments, and wasted time.

Be sure to plan how you will **check for understanding** after explaining directions, procedures, rules, etc. For example, you may ask specific questions — What do you do first? How do you find your partner? — and/or call on individuals to summarize the directions. Simply saying — Does everyone understand? or Any questions? — is *not* effective.

Component 4 - Activity Closing

The activity *closing* helps students tie it all together. Decide whether it will be important to review key ideas and to preview future lessons or activities. It may be necessary to provide an opportunity for students to draw conclusions; to describe their problem solving process; or to show what they created. You may wish to formally assess progress toward a long-term objective. Activity closings do not necessarily need to be time consuming and elaborate, but there should be a meaningful ending of some kind for all activities.

Component 5 - Editing Tasks

Once you have written the activity plan, reread it and evaluate whether you have planned the following:

- *for equipment and materials you will need for the activity.* Are these readily available in the classroom? If not, how will you locate them?

- *for all necessary logistics* — distribution of materials, safe use of equipment, clean-up, etc. What will assistants be doing, and will you need extra help to implement the activity, such as parent volunteers? If so, how and when will you arrange for this help?

- *for behavior management* — clarification of behavior rules and expectations; explanation of positive and negative consequences; presentation of what students should do if they finish early, etc.

- *for diversity* — active responding, peer helpers, etc. (See Chapter 6 for additional diversity strategies.)

Write any additions in the appropriate section of your plan.

SUMMARY

There are many types of activities to plan for your students, and they should all have a clear purpose. Be sure you can state the important goal or objective that the activity will help your students meet.

Figure 4.1 summarizes each component in an activity plan. Notice that Components 1 and 5 are different in that they are not presented to the students. Instead, they ask you to think through the goal of your activity and to make sure you have included strategies to make your activity go smoothly. When you write your activity plan, first write Component 1, next Component 3, then Components 2 and 4, and last Component 5.

* * * * * * * * * * * * * * * * * * * *

STUDY SUGGESTIONS

1. Look up the following terms in the appendix:

    activity goal
    activity rationale
    signal for attention
    statement of behavior expectations
    opening
    active participation
    check for understanding
    closing

2. Read the sample activity plans at the end of this chapter. *Important*: Notice that complete sentences are used in many parts of the plans. This is to help you follow/understand as you read them. When you write your own plans, use phrases and abbreviations whenever possible.

3. Write an activity plan. See the activity examples in Chapter 2 for ideas for topics.

Figure 4.1 WRITING AN ACTIVITY PLAN

The content of the components below tells what typically would be included in each component in an activity plan. When you write your plan, clearly label each component; e.g., Component 1 - Preplanning Tasks, and its parts; e.g., activity goal, activity rationale.

Component 1 - <u>PREPLANNING TASKS</u>

<u>Write</u>:
- ✎ the *activity goal* — What is the intended learning outcome? If the purpose of the activity is to provide practice toward a long-term objective, write that objective here.
- ✎ the *activity rationale* — Why is this an important goal?

Component 2 - <u>ACTIVITY BEGINNING</u>

<u>Write</u>:
- ✎ a *signal for attention* to make sure students are listening.
- ✎ a *statement of behavior expectations* to inform students how to act during the activity.
- ✎ an *opening* to show students how this activity connects to yesterday's lesson, to personal experiences, or to prior knowledge and/or to motivate/focus the students; e.g., stating the activity rationale.

Component 3 - <u>ACTIVITY MIDDLE</u>

<u>Write</u>:
- ✎ a description of *what* you need to communicate to the students. You may need one or a combination of the following, depending on the type of activity:
  - ✓ a set of questions   ✓ a list of statements/explanations   ✓ a list of rules
  - ✓ a list of procedures   ✓ a sample of a finished product   ✓ a list of directions
- ✎ a description of *how* you will effectively communicate this information to the students — use of *visual aids*, demonstrations, *checks for understanding*, *active participation*, etc.

Component 4 - <u>ACTIVITY CLOSING</u>

<u>Write</u>:
- ✎ a description of how you will end the activity. Your *closing* may include one or more of the following:
  - ✓ class review   ✓ students draw conclusions   ✓ teacher previews future learning
  - ✓ students show work   ✓ evaluation procedure (if appropriate) is implemented

---

Component 5 - <u>EDITING TASKS</u>

<u>Write</u> (in the appropriate sections of your plan):
- ✎ a list of necessary materials
- ✎ logistics
- ✎ behavior management plans
- ✎ diversity strategies

SAMPLE ACTIVITY PLAN #1

Topic: MATH BINGO

PREPLANNING TASKS

<u>Activity Goal</u>: Students will increase accuracy and fluency on addition facts with sums from 10-20. They are working toward the long-term objective: Students will write answers to addition facts (0-20) at the rate of 80 digits per minute with 0 errors.

<u>Activity Rationale</u>: Accuracy and fluency on addition facts is an important basic math skill. The game format is intended to provide variety in practice and to increase interest and motivation.

<u>Materials and Logistics</u>: Put cards and markers on desks while students are at recess. Put flashcards with sums 10-20 in a bowl. Set up an overhead projector.

ACTIVITY BEGINNING

Signal for attention: "Give me 5!"

Opening:
Say: "Today we're going to practice addition facts by playing Math Bingo. You remember how to play Bingo; we've done that before. We're going to use that game to practice addition facts so you can reach your math goals faster."

Behavior expectations: "Stay in your seats, but you may talk quietly during the game."

ACTIVITY MIDDLE

The class has played Bingo before, and they know the basic rules.

Say: "Listen carefully while I tell you the directions for the game."
Show: A poster with directions summarized on it.
Show and Tell: Demonstrate while explaining directions.

1. The caller will pull a card from the bowl and read the addition problem on it; write the answer (from the back of card) on the overhead which is not turned on; set the card aside.
2. Players think of the answer in your heads. (If you didn't hear the problem, raise your hand for a repeat.)
3. Look for the answer on your cards.
4. If the answer is on your card, put a marker on it.
5. When you get a row filled in, call out "Bingo." (Briefly remind the class of three ways to get a row: horizontally, vertically, or diagonally.)

ACTIVITY MIDDLE (continued)

6. The caller turns on the overhead, and the desk partner helps the player check for accuracy of BINGO. Remind the player not to completely remove the markers in case the game goes on. The rest of the players don't dump cards yet. If a tie, both check cards.
7. If there's a winner, start a new game. The winner becomes the caller.
   If there's not a winner, continue the game.
   If there's a tie, the person whose name is first in the alphabet becomes the caller. (The teacher is the first caller.)

Say: "We'll play until 10:30. We'll stop then even if in the middle of a game."

Quickly restate the directions; *check for understanding* by asking for unison responses to questions; e.g., "Where does the caller write the answer?"

Briefly remind the class of previously learned strategies to use if they can't think of the answer in their heads; i.e., count-ups, fingers, counting beans, and scratch paper. (Make sure Stan and Bettie have their counting beans out and both have peer helpers.)

Say: "Get ready for the first game." Draw the first problem and then continue until there is a winner.

Next games: Stand near a new caller to prompt on the procedures for the first problem or two.

Monitor to look for specific addition facts that students are having difficulty with and jot them down on the clipboard.

ACTIVITY CLOSING

Signal for attention: "Give me five!"

Ask the two class "helpers" to collect cards and markers and put them in the box. While they are doing this . . . . Review difficult problems found during monitoring; e.g., say "6 plus 7 equals 13; What is 6 + 7, everyone?; Yes, say it with me . . . 6 + 7 = 13."

Remind students of flash card practice or computer practice as a free time activity in the math center and at home.

EDITING TASKS

Stan and Bettie will need help with accuracy of the answers to addition facts (noted within the plan). Switch lights on and off if the noise level gets too high. (Students know this signal.)

SAMPLE ACTIVITY PLAN #2

Topic: THE UNDERGROUND RAILROAD

PREPLANNING TASKS

Note: The after lunch story is used to give more breadth to topics being studied in other curricular areas; e.g., social studies. Currently we are studying immigration and why various groups of people came to America. We have begun our study of citizens of African American descent and are investigating the issues that lead up to the abolition of slavery.

Activity Goal: Students will understand the contributions that Harriet Tubman made to helping many slaves escape to freedom. Secondarily, students will learn about a complex system — the Underground Railroad — that was set up to help people escape the bondage of slavery.

Activity Rationale: The rationale for the activity goal is that as citizens we must know about and learn from our history. Understanding some of the issues surrounding slavery in this country helps students to better understand racial tensions that exist even today. It is also important that students learn about individuals who risk so much because they are committed to improving the human condition — these are positive role models. Harriet Tubman was one such individual.

Materials and Logistics: Need *Traveling on the Underground Railroad* by Steven Everett — this is an imaginary book and author — and vocabulary words written on the board before the activity.

ACTIVITY BEGINNING

Signal for attention: Count backwards, "5, 4, 3, 2, 1!" Wait until everyone is looking.

Statement of behavior expectations: Stay in seats, look, and listen.
Opening:
(connecting statements) SAY: We have been studying the reasons why various groups of individuals traveled to America. Yesterday we talked about how the arrival of African Americans was unique. They came here not by choice, but rather by force. Their arrival in America did not represent an escape to "the land of the free" but rather the beginning of a life of slavery . . . property of "masters" living in the South, being dreadfully mistreated.

(focusing statements) SAY: Thankfully, as you know, a significant number of slaves made it to freedom because of the Underground Railroad (U.R.). Today you will hear more about Harriet Tubman and how she helped slaves escape on this railroad. You'll also learn about how the U.R. worked.

The U.R. was not really a railroad. It was the name used to describe all of the secret places, routes, and ways by which slaves traveled to escape from captivity in the South.

ACTIVITY MIDDLE

Reminders to myself:

‣ Draw NAME STICKS to help ensure that a variety of students answer questions.
‣ Mark whole class behavior points throughout activity when ALL students are following directions.

Say: "There are some very specific vocabulary words that will help you better understand how the U.R. worked. I've written each word and its definition on the board."

Review terms: Leave on board for students to use as a reference. (**diversity strategy**)

> <u>underground railroad</u> - the name used to describe all of the secret places, routes, and ways by which slaves traveled to escape from captivity in the South
> <u>conductor</u> - guides
> <u>station or depot</u> - business or home where slaves were hidden
> <u>passengers</u> - the runaway slaves

Say: "You will need to listen carefully as I read this story to you. You'll hear what it was like to be a slave; how the U.R. got started; and how it worked. You will also hear about Harriet Tubman and why she is to be so admired."

"Before I read each section of the story to you, I'll tell you what information you should listen for. I'll stop at the end of each section and ask questions about that information." (**diversity strategy**)

BEGIN READING: I'll walk around as I read and stand near those who have trouble attending. (**diversity strategy**)

1. <u>Section 1 - pgs. 1-6</u>
   before reading
   Say: "Listen to find out why the slaves wanted to run away; why they were punished."

   after reading
   Ask: "What kinds of 'offenses' were the slaves punished for?"
   "Why did the slaves want to run away to the North?"
   Have students discuss answers with <u>table groups</u>; use NAME STICKS.

2. <u>Section 2 - pgs. 7-12</u>
   before reading
   Say: "Listen to find out how the U.R. worked and what the various parts of the U.R. were."
   Refer to key terms on the board.

   after reading
   Ask: "How did the U.R. work?"
   " What were the roles of the conductor and of the stations?"
   " What was a typical trip on the U.R. like?"
   Have students discuss answers with <u>partner</u>; use NAME STICKS.

30

ACTIVITY MIDDLE (continued)

3. Section 3 - pgs. 13-20
    before reading
    Say: "Find out how and when Harriet Tubman first used the U.R."

    after reading
    Ask: "What events led to Harriet Tubman's first trip on the U.R.?"
    " What was the scariest part of her trip?"
    Have students discuss answers with <u>table group</u>; use NAME STICKS.

4. Section 4 - pgs. 21-34
    before reading
    Say: "You will learn how and why Harriet Tubman became involved in helping others use the U.R."

    after reading
    Ask: "Harriet Tubman decided to help others use the U.R. Why?"
    "Why did she continue to help for so long even though it was so dangerous?"
    Have students discuss answers with <u>partner</u>; use NAME STICKS.

ACTIVITY ENDING

Tell students they will be doing a follow-up writing assignment about H. Tubman and the U.R. They'll need facts to use so . . .

Have them construct a concept map with as many facts as possible about U.R. and Harriet Tubman. (They frequently use concept maps as a way to organize facts and information as a review.) GIVE THEM THREE MINUTES TO WRITE; then give them two minutes to compare with a neighbor.

EDITING TASKS

<u>specific management</u> - class points for following directions.
<u>individual accommodations</u> - Keep Michelle close to me so I can keep her on task. Have Ellen help Paul fill in his map.

Topic: DAILY OPENING ROUTINE (elementary grades)

A SPECIAL TYPE OF ACTIVITY PLAN

The objectives to be accomplished through the use of the daily morning opening activities are generally long-term objectives/goals — counting by 1s, 5s, 10s to 100; correct punctuation of sentences; etc. The daily activities themselves provide practice for students on the way to meeting long-term objectives. A teacher would generally not attempt to monitor each student during "opening" activities as a means of evaluating individual performance in relation to the long-term objectives. (However, you may want to focus on one or two students each day for informal evaluation of progress.) In addition, a teacher would not expect that any one of the long-term objectives would be reached at the end of one day's activities.

A typical activity plan may not work well for the "opening" activities in many classrooms. "Opening" often consists of a series of activities which occur in the same order each day; e.g., lunch count, attendance, a geography or history challenge question, math puzzlers, etc. It may be difficult to fit these activities into a typical activity plan.

A more useful plan for "opening" is simply a list of the activities with specific information included as needed. Long-term objectives and an activity rationale should be incorporated as appropriate. It will save time if you design a "form" (and make multiple copies) that can be used for opening. You can simply leave space for writing in the information that changes from day to day; for example, the geography challenge question. A sample activity plan for opening activities in an elementary classroom follows. The information written in bold print would be changed every day; e.g., the day and date, the Language Mix-Up sentences, the attendance taker, etc.

DAILY OPENING

Date: **Monday, September 6**

BEFORE SCHOOL: Write the Language Mix-Up sentences and daily schedule on the board.

8:50 - Students begin coming into the classroom.

1. Language Mix-Up: Sentences are on the board and the students begin working on them at their desks. *Note*: Language Mix-Up is a program in which students are given sentences, every day, that have errors in them. Students must find and correct the errors.

Long-Term Objective(s) for Language Mix-Up: Students will (1) write complete sentences — with subject and verb — that ask and tell; (2) use the period, question mark, and exclamation point correctly in all writing; (3) apply capitalization rules — sentence beginning, proper nouns — in all writing.

Daily Activity Rationale: Language Mix-Up provides students daily practice with identification and correction of errors in sentence construction, grammar, and punctuation.

Today's Language Mix-Up Practice: **Practice on (1) capitalizing proper nouns and sentence beginnings; and (2) use of question marks and periods.**

Language Mix-Up sentences for today are:

> **molly and her sister leah run rapidly down the street?**
> **did you know that dr. cook was a very good dentist.**

9:00 - FIRST BELL RINGS

2. Take Attendance: Call on the class "helper of the day" to take attendance.

helper   _____**Morelia**_____

3. Lunch Count: The teacher takes the lunch count. Students stand in the following order: hot lunch, milk. Then, the "helper" takes the attendance report and lunch count to the office.

9:05 - LAST BELL RINGS

4. Flag Salute: Have the class weekly "leader" lead the flag salute.

leader   _____**Robby**_____

5. <u>Daily Schedule</u>: The teacher reads and explains the daily schedule to the students.

   Special Event: Explain about the fire safety assembly scheduled for 9:30 — a fire truck is being brought to the school and students will be able to climb up on the truck. Explain the rules.

   a) **Five students may be on the truck at one time.**
   b) **Students will be selected by the teacher — five at a time — until everyone has had a turn.**
   c) **Students must follow the directions of the fire fighters. This is for safety reasons.**
   d) **Students not on the truck will be able to look at the fire equipment.**

9:10

6. <u>Language Mix-Up Corrections</u>: Call on a different student (DRAW NAMES) for each correction, and have students make corrections right on the overhead. Have other students stand up/sit down or thumbs up/thumbs down to show they agree or disagree. Ask questions — such as, "Why did you capitalize the word Leah? Everyone . . . ?" Use unison responses to emphasize rules — such as, ". . . because names begin with capital letters."

9:15

7. <u>Sharing</u>: Opportunities to share are given on a rotating basis. The "Sharing Chart" should be checked to see who has had the opportunity to share and who is next. In case of an absence, the next student on the chart may be chosen.

Chapter 5

Lesson Plans

INTRODUCTION

Planning daily lessons is the end result of a complex planning process done by a teacher. This process begins when the teacher determines the overall curriculum to be taught. The curriculum is based on an analysis of student needs, on district or state standards, and/or on a student's Individualized Education Program (IEP). Once the curriculum for the year or for a particular unit is identified, the teacher divides the content into individual lessons and writes specific lesson objectives, making sure each lesson clearly fits with the goals of the overall curriculum. The teacher finally selects a lesson model — e.g., direct instruction, informal presentation — that will work best to meet the objective of a specific lesson.

Teachers use lessons to help students attain a specific short term objective. Lessons typically have a clear beginning and ending, and they will last a few hours at the most. Lessons are followed by an evaluation of each student's learning in relation to the selected objective(s). Series of lessons that lead to the attainment of long term objectives or goals are often combined into a unit of instruction.

Lessons can be used to teach specific skills and information directly or to give students the opportunity to discover information on their own or with their peers. The type of content that can be taught through lessons is extremely diverse. Teachers typically use lessons to teach academic content; to develop study skills, social skills, and problem-solving skills; and to promote higher level thinking.

The following objectives help demonstrate the wide variety of skills and knowledge that can be addressed in lessons.

▶ When teased in a role-playing situation, students will "talk through" each of the five problem-solving steps.

▶ On a worksheet of 25 sentences, students will circle the complete subject in all sentences.

▶ Given a list of ten assignments, students will accurately transfer all of them to an assignment calendar.

▶ Using the written strategy as a reference, students will independently outline one social studies text chapter. The outline must include all headings, subheadings, and at least three details for each subheading.

GENERIC COMPONENTS OF A LESSON PLAN

A lesson plan is a written description of how students will progress toward a specific objective. It clearly describes the teaching behavior — e.g., statements and actions — that it is hoped will result in student learning.

All lesson plans include the following eight generic components: preplanning tasks, lesson set-up, lesson opening, lesson body, lesson closing, extended practice, evaluation, and editing tasks. The specific content of the components will vary with different lesson models because each model enables students to progress toward an object in a different way.

The following descriptions of each component include two parts: the purpose and a summary of the type of content that could be used. Our intent is to help you generate ideas, not to list everything that must be included in each component in every lesson plan. It is up to you to select and/or generate the specifics that are appropriate for the lesson model, the subject matter, and the students being taught. As you plan each component, be sure to include diversity strategies. (See Chapter 6.)

The components are described here in the order in which they would appear in the lesson plan. This is not necessarily the order in which they will be written. When preparing to write a lesson plan, refer to Figure 5.1 for a suggested writing sequence and to Chapters 7-10 for information about the specific model you will be using.

Component 1 - Preplanning Tasks

The purpose of this component is to help you thoroughly think through the content to be taught and the best way to teach it. Generally, this component consists of the following:

- Content Analysis - The first step in this component is to decide on the specific content to be taught. This is accomplished by completing a thorough *content analysis*. This analysis helps you think in detail about the content you will be teaching, which in turn allows you to determine the best way for the content to be taught.

The term content analysis is a general one. The various types of content analysis are: a *subject matter outline*, a *task analysis* or a *concept analysis*, definitions of *key terms/vocabulary*, and a list of *prerequisite skills/knowledge*.

The type of content analysis done depends on *what* is being taught. When you plan to teach a concept for example, the content analysis will always consist of at least a concept analysis. When the point of the lesson is to teach a skill or procedure, you would always include a task analysis. When teaching information about a topic, a subject matter outline works best. All lessons may have a number of key terms and vocabulary that need to be defined in ways the students would understand. Prerequisite skills and knowledge would also be routinely considered as part of a content analysis. This analysis will help determine whether the content is appropriate for the students and will also help you write the objective.

- Objective - Select and write a clear, specific, worthwhile lesson objective. The *objective(s)* must contain a behavior, the content, the condition, and the criterion so that you can specify, in detail, what is to be learned and how well the students are to learn it. (See Chapter 3.)

- Objective Rationale - Once you have written the objective, you need to decide if it, in fact, represents an important learning outcome appropriate for your students. This can be done by asking yourself questions such as the following: "Why is this objective important?" "Is this something my students can use in the future?" Do my students have the necessary prerequisite skills or knowledge needed to be successful with this objective?" When you are satisfied with your answers to these questions, you will have an *objective rationale*.

- Lesson Model - Now you are ready to determine the best way to teach to the objective. This decision can be based on the objective itself, the students, the time available, and/or the type of content being taught — e.g., very abstract or difficult. Lesson models presented in this text are direct instruction, informal presentation, and structured discovery.

Note: Sometimes practicum students and student teachers make the mistake of selecting activities and methods before the objective is written. This sequence can lead to trying to figure out an objective in order to fit the activity. For example, "This activity seems like fun.....I wonder what the purpose of it is?" The lesson process must be congruent with the objective of the lesson, specifically, and with the curriculum, generally.

Component 2 - Lesson Set-Up

The purpose of the *lesson set-up* is to prepare students for the beginning of the lesson. A lesson should not begin until you have the students' attention — i.e., they are physically turned toward you, they are listening to you, etc. Also, problems can be prevented by explaining behavior expectations to students right up front, rather than waiting for problems to occur.

- Signal for Attention - A signal is used to gain students' attention by having them look at you and listen to you so the lesson can begin. In some cases, students are ready and a simple "Let's get started" or "Good morning" is a sufficient *signal for attention*. In other cases a stronger signal — such as turning the lights off/on or ringing a bell — is needed to attract their attention. It is necessary to wait for everyone's attention and to acknowledge it.

- Statement of Behavior Expectations - This is the explanation of the rules — i.e., how you expect the students to act during the lesson. It is not necessary to review *all* classroom rules, just those most pertinent to the current lesson; e.g., raising hands, getting help. The *statement of behavior expectations* should be written in language that is positive, is appropriate to the age of the students, is specific, and is clear. You should consider stating expectations at each transition within the lesson, rather that stating them all at the beginning.

Component 3 - Lesson Opening

The purpose of the lesson *opening* is to help prepare the students' minds for the learning to come. You will typically want to let students know what they're going to learn; why it's important; and how it builds on what they already know. You will also want to get them excited about learning. Planning the lesson opening consists of selecting one or more strategies from each of the following categories:

- Motivate and/or Focus Students - The following are some ways to motivate and/or focus students: tell or show the lesson objective (*state the objective*); use an attention-getting "set;" tell the purpose, rationale, importance, or application of the lesson objective (*objective purpose*).

- Connect New Learning - The following are some ways that you can help students see relationships between known information and the new learning: discuss how the learning connects to personal experience and prior knowledge; review earlier lessons or skills; preview upcoming lessons; present an *advance organizer*; show a *graphic organizer*.

Component 4 - Lesson Body

The initial instruction, related directly to the lesson objective, occurs in the *lesson body*. For this reason, Component 4 is considered the "heart" of the lesson. Most of the planning time and most of the teaching time is spent on the lesson body. The specifics of the body will depend on the lesson model selected. (See Chapters 7-10.)

The lesson body describes specific statements you will make and actions you will take. The teaching that is described in the lesson body should be obvious to anyone reading your plan. Enough detail should be included so that someone else could teach the lesson just by following your plan.

Diversity strategies, practice activities, and monitoring student progress strategies will also be included in the lesson body.

Component 5 - Extended Practice

The purpose of the *extended practice* component is to plan for the development of high enough levels of accuracy and fluency to ensure that students can generalize the skill or knowledge. Students will usually need extended practice opportunities prior to evaluation. These opportunities are provided through activities, seatwork, and homework. Monitoring practice activities will help determine when students are ready to be evaluated. Decisions will have to be made about the following:

- Practice Opportunities - Describe the plan for providing practice opportunities during and following the lesson. These are in addition to initial practice provided during the body of the lesson. Remember that some students may need a great deal of extended practice while others may need enrichment activities. Be sure that students have an opportunity to practice *individually* prior to evaluation.

- Related Lessons or Activities - It is useful to determine and list which other lessons or activities will build on this objective and/or provide opportunities to generalize and/or extend the information.

Component 6 - Lesson Closing

The lesson *closing* helps students tie it all together. It may follow the body of the lesson, or it may follow extended practice. Lesson closings can be elaborate or simple, but there always needs to be one.

A lesson closing may include one or more of the following: a review of the key points of the lesson; some opportunities for students to draw conclusions; a preview of future learning; a description of where or when students should use their new skills or knowledge; a time for students to show their work; a reference to the lesson opening.

Component 7 - Evaluation

The purpose of the *evaluation* component is to let you and your students know if learning has occurred. It also helps you determine whether it is appropriate to build on the current lesson or whether you need to reteach or change the lesson model, activities, or materials.

The lesson evaluation was actually planned when the lesson objective was written. Look back at the objective(s) to be sure the evaluation matches the objective, and then describe when and where the evaluation will occur. For example, if the objective was "to write a paragraph with a topic sentence," you might plan to have the students write the paragraph tomorrow morning in class. Regardless of when you ask them to write it, they may *not* be the practice paragraphs they wrote with peer help and/or your help. Remember that evaluations need to be of *each* individual student's *independent* performance. Do not confuse teaching and testing.

Monitoring the students during the body of the lesson and/or during extended practice will give you an idea of when to formally evaluate. There is no sense in giving students a test that you know they will fail. Students may be evaluated again later; e.g., on a unit test. They may also be evaluated on an on-going basis. For example, you could evaluate paragraph construction in their journal writing. Learning must always be evaluated following the lesson, regardless of other evaluations planned. This evaluation is essential for deciding what to teach next.

Component 8 - Editing Tasks

The purpose of this component is to help you examine and complete the first lesson draft. When this component is finished, the lesson plan will be complete — all necessary adjustments will have been made in order to help ensure that all students will be challenged and successful.

- Examine Lesson Congruence - It is imperative that the various components in the lesson match; i.e., the body of the lesson and the evaluation must both match the lesson objective. The following is an example of a lesson in which *none* of the components match:

  objective = write sentences which include adjectives
  teaching = teacher shows and tells how to identify adjectives in a sentence
  practice = students are asked to list adjectives which describe a given object
  evaluation = students write definition of adjective

To determine lesson congruence, ask yourself the following questions:

1. Am I teaching the information specified in the objective?
2. Am I testing what I taught?
3. Does my evaluation match my objective?

- Examine Diversity Strategies - The lesson plan must be designed to meet the needs of diverse learners. Therefore, strategies must be written directly into the plan. (See Chapter 6.)

- Managing Student Behavior - Sometimes great lessons fall apart because student behavior has not been considered in the lesson plan equation. Management problems can be prevented by planning ahead for how partners should work together; for distributing materials; for transitions between activities within lessons; etc. This increases chances of lesson success. Therefore, after the lesson plan has been written, it is necessary to go back through it and write in specific management strategies. Ask yourself the following questions:

1. Do I need to do additional management planning because of the kinds of things I am doing in the lesson; e.g., lots of equipment and material needed, many transitions within the lesson?

2. Do I need to do additional management planning because of the needs of the students; e.g., incorporate stronger reinforcement, re-arrange seats, select partners, use precorrection plans, etc.?

- Materials/Equipment - The final task in this component is to decide what special or unusual materials and/or equipment is needed for the lesson. It may make sense to list only those materials and/or equipment not readily available in the classroom. Items such as pencils and paper would not need to appear on the materials list, whereas a hot plate, test tubes, or waxed paper probably would.

STEPS IN WRITING A LESSON PLAN

Writing a lesson plan requires a series of decisions. Even before starting to write the actual lesson plan, decisions must be made about what exactly is to be taught and how to best teach it. Experienced teachers are able to do more thinking and less writing when they plan lessons because of their experience. They do, however, often write fairly detailed plans when they prepare to teach new content. This helps them to think through what is the best way to teach the information they will present.

Clearly written, detailed lesson plans increase the chances that a lesson will be successful. A preservice or beginning teacher will spend a lot of time writing detailed lesson plans because much of what is taught will be new material. The best way to become fluent in writing lesson plans is to *practice* writing them. As experience grows, the teacher will need to write less because certain aspects of the lessons will become second-nature.

All of the generic components presented in this chapter should be included in every written lesson plan until you gain the necessary experience to reduce your written planning. The order in which the various components of the plan are written, however, does not necessarily correspond to the order in which they appear in this chapter or to the order in which they would be presented to the students. For example, it makes more sense to write the lesson body before the lesson opening, but, when the lesson is presented to the students, you would obviously present the lesson opening before the lesson body. It is also important to note that, although Components 2-7 are the only ones actually presented to the students, the preplanning and editing components are equally important and should be completed in writing.

The steps to follow when writing a lesson plan are the same regardless of the model being used for teaching. Figure 5.1 provides a summary of a logical sequence that can be followed when lesson plans are written; it can be used for all lesson models.

Note: Chapters 7-10 contain detailed information about writing specific types of plans.

* * * * * * * * * * * * * * * * * * * *

Figure 5.1 STEPS IN WRITING A LESSON PLAN

Remember to think about diversity strategies as you plan each component of your lesson plan.

COMPLETE COMPONENT 1 (Preplanning Tasks)
  1. *Write* a content analysis.
  2. *Write* a lesson objective(s).
  3. *Write* an objective rationale.
  4. *Determine* the lesson model to be used.

COMPLETE COMPONENTS 3-7 IN THE FOLLOWING ORDER:
  5. *Write* Component 4 (Lesson Body).
  6. *Write* Component 5 (Extended Practice).
  7. *Write* Component 7 (Evaluation).
  8. *Write* Component 3 (Lesson Opening).
  9. *Write* Component 6 (Lesson Closing).

COMPLETE COMPONENT 8 (Editing Tasks)
  10. *Evaluate* lesson congruence. Ask yourself, "Do the objective, lesson body, extended practice, and evaluation all match?"
  11. *Evaluate* the use of diversity strategies. (See Chapter 6 for ideas.)
  12. *Write* specific management strategies.
  13. *Write* a list of materials/equipment needed for the lesson.

COMPLETE COMPONENT 2 (Lesson Set-Up)
  14. *Write* a signal for attention.
  15. *Write* a statement of behavior expectations.

STUDY SUGGESTION

Check your understanding of these terms by referring to the appendix.

advance organizer	objective
closing	objective purpose
concept analysis	objective rationale
content analysis	opening
evaluation	prerequisite skills/knowledge
extended practice	signal for attention
graphic organizer	statement of behavior expectations
key terms/vocabulary	state the objective
lesson body	subject matter outline
lesson set-up	task analysis

REFERENCES

Arends, R.I. *Classroom Instruction and Management*. New York: McGraw-Hill, 1997.

Borich, G. *Effective Teaching Methods*. 2nd ed. New York: Merrill, an imprint of Macmillan Publishing Company, 1991.

Cartwright, P.G., C.A. Cartwright, and M.E. Ward. *Educating Special Learners*. 4th ed. Boston: Wadsworth Publishing Company, 1995.

Clark, L.H., and I.S. Starr. *Secondary and Middle School Teaching Methods*. 6th ed. New York: Macmillan Publishing Company, 1991.

Lorber, M.A., and W.D. Pierce. *Objectives, Methods, and Evaluation for Secondary Teaching*. 3rd ed. Englewood Cliffs: Prentice Hall, 1990.

Chapter 6

Diversity Strategies

INTRODUCTION

Classrooms are made up of highly diverse individuals. They may include students from a variety of cultural and linguistic backgrounds; students with varied gifts and talents; students with different kinds of disabilities; and students with learning and behavior problems. This diversity means that teachers need to incorporate those teaching strategies, in their activity and lesson plans, which increase the likelihood that all students will be successful. In addition to preparing lessons for the entire class, teachers need to plan individual accommodations to address the diversity among students. This chapter is intended to provide a variety of suggestions or "diversity strategies" to consider as lessons and activities are being planned for students. These strategies or suggestions are divided into three parts.

In Part 1, suggestions are categorized by the planning components described in Chapter 4 (Activity Plans) and Chapter 5 (Lesson Plans). These strategies are to be incorporated into the initial planning. The suggestions will help in the following ways:

▸ to make teaching and management generally effective; e.g., everyone will benefit if the new learning is connected to prior knowledge.

▸ to incorporate variety into teaching and management in order to make it more likely that all students will be reached; e.g., use different lesson models.

▸ to include strategies which may be essential for the success of some students, while being helpful to all of the students; e.g., use of mnemonics.

In Part 2, strategies are categorized by "problem;" e.g., when students have difficulty maintaining attention or difficulty beginning tasks. Whether these suggestions are incorporated into initial planning for the whole class or used as individual accommodations for certain students depends on the make-up of the class. These suggestions focus on mild to moderate learning and behavior problems and do not include accommodations necessary for severe and low incidence disabilities. (For ease in locating ideas, strategies may be listed under more than one category in Part 1 and Part 2.)

In Part 3, strategies are provided which help plan for the cultural diversity of students. There are suggestions about the content of lessons and activities and about methods of instruction and management which are meant to help foster the involvement and success of students from diverse cultural backgrounds.

AN EXAMPLE OF PLANNING FOR DIVERSITY

The following example shows many ways that teachers may incorporate diversity strategies into their teaching.

Mrs. Troxel plans an activity in which her students are asked to create new endings to a story. The

42

intention is to provide additional practice on making inferences, following reading comprehension instruction. She will read the first half of the story to the students and then they will write their own endings.

▸ Mrs. Troxel begins by helping students connect their prior knowledge and experience to this activity — an effective teaching strategy which she considers important for the learning of all students. She does this by helping students connect their use of inferences and predictions in every day situations through asking questions such as, "You see pork, onions, green chiles, and tortillas on the grocery list. What do you think you'll have for supper? What is another possibility?"

▸ During her initial planning of this activity, Mrs. Troxel automatically decides to provide both written and oral directions for writing the story endings. She knows that this is essential for several of her students and that many of them find it helpful. (She also finds that going through the process of writing directions herself results in clearer directions and ends up saving instructional time.)

▸ Many of Mrs. Troxel's students have difficulty completing tasks. When planning the activity, Mrs. Troxel specifies the criteria for a completed story ending assignment — finish ending, proofread ending, put name on paper, place in box on back table — and decides to list these on the blackboard. She has incorporated this strategy into her initial planning, rather than as a separate accommodation, since the make-up of her class makes this sensible.

▸ Two of Mrs. Troxel's students have serious writing problems. The accommodation she plans for them is to dictate their story endings into a tape recorder. She chooses not to have all of her students dictate their endings, because she finds it more convenient to read papers than to listen to tapes and because she

wants to provide many writing opportunities for her class.

▸ When Mrs. Troxel selects the story for which the students will create endings, she chooses a story by a Mexican American author. She wants her students to identify with authors and tries to promote this by choosing stories written by people with similar ethnic backgrounds to those of her students.

▸ Some of the students in Mrs. Troxel's class are more productive when they have the opportunity to work with peers; others prefer to work alone. This may be related to cultural background. Mrs. Troxel decides that the students may, or may not, choose to consult peers when writing their story endings.

The goal when planning for diversity is to help all students be successful. It is also important to be realistic about time demands. Typically, it is more efficient to incorporate diversity strategies into initial planning, rather than try to plan many individual accommodations after the fact.

This chapter is a brief summary or review of some of the many strategies recommended in the literature for helping students learn (Algozzine and Ysseldyke, 1992; Cegelka and Berdine, 1995; Cummings, 1990; Evertson, Emmer, Clements, and Worsham, 1994; Fisher, Schumaker, and Deshler, 1995; Lovitt, 1995; Meltzer, et al., 1996; Prater, 1992; Sprick, Sprick, and Garrison, 1992). It is essential to monitor the progress of individual students to assess whether the strategies are working; i.e., the student is learning. More specialized accommodations will be necessary for some students.

Note: A common concern of teachers these days is the number of students who have difficulties with inattention, impulsiveness, and over activity and who may or may not have the label of ADD or ADHD. We're not going to deal here with issues of labeling, over-diagnosis, use of drugs, and so on. Instead, we have included suggestions for

43

strategies which can help students pay attention, wait, and modulate activity levels. Some may be appropriate as part of whole class planning and some as adaptations for individuals.

PART 1
DIVERSITY STRATEGIES
BY PLANNING COMPONENT

As you engage in initial planning of activities and lessons, consider the diversity strategies you can incorporate in each component of the plan to help all students succeed.

Planning Components

- content
- objective
- model
- signal for attention
- behavior expectations
- opening
- body or middle
- extended practice
- closing
- evaluation
- management
- materials

When Planning the Content

— Be sure that you are teaching important knowledge and skills. If students have fallen behind in the curriculum, there is no time for fluff and filler. Teach what is most generalizable.

— Consider the possibility that you need to teach more lessons and fewer activities. Reexamine the rationale for the planned activities.

— Select content based on the students' interests. Offer choices to students when possible. For example, allow students to read articles from the sports pages in order to practice reading skills.

— Teach students to set and monitor their own learning goals.

— Teach learning strategies along with teaching content areas; e.g., work on active reading strategies in the social studies textbook.

— Teach school survival/task-related skills; e.g., social skills, study skills, test-taking skills, problem solving skills, organizational skills.

— Teach students the skills they need to be successful in various teaching models and methods; e.g., discussion skills, peer interaction skills.

— Teach the behavior you expect students to display in the classroom; e.g., procedures and routines for making transitions, for asking for help, for turning in homework, for cleaning up.

When Planning the Objective

— Pretest to make sure the objective is appropriate for the students.

— Examine the criterion. Is it at the right level? Basic skills which are prerequisites for higher level skills, need high criterion levels. For example, 100% accuracy is necessary for letter recognition because that is an important basic skill needed for acquiring later skills. On the other hand, 100% accuracy in distinguishing reptiles from amphibians may not be necessary.

— Examine the condition. Is it realistic? Students may be more motivated to reach objectives when they can see the "real world" application.

— After analyzing prerequisite skills, the objective for individual students may need to be altered. For example, could students who have poor writing skills demonstrate that they can recognize the key conflict in a short story by saying it rather than writing it? Could students who are inaccurate on multiplication facts demonstrate that they know how to find the area of a rectangle using a calculator? In other words, the purpose is to allow the student to go on learning — not to be held back by those writing or multiplication difficulties. On the other hand, in most cases the student continues to need instruction and practice on writing and multiplication.

— Do not rush to make changes in the curriculum for students with learning problems. Changes may affect success in upper grades or, in the long term, options for employment or further schooling. Having a student draw a picture or sing a song rather than write a paragraph may provide momentary success, but it is unlikely to be an option offered by future employers.

When Deciding on the Model and Methods

— Recognize that students with learning and behavior problems often require very explicit instruction. This needs to be followed by focused, active practice with immediate feedback.

— Evaluate the level of structure that the students need to be successful. Do not assume that all students learn best with, or even prefer, unstructured approaches.

— If the students have fallen behind in the curriculum, use models and methods which are most time efficient.

— Evaluate the amount of academic learning time that each student would have in the lesson or activity. For example, having groups of students work together to bake cookies may sound like a good way to practice measurement skills. However, when you look closely, you may see that, in an hour long activity, Joanne spent thirty seconds measuring one tablespoon of cinnamon. Not much practice!

— Be sure that students have the necessary skills to be successful in the methods you are using. For example, can they share materials or reach consensus if you are using small group projects?

These skills may need to be directly taught in advance. In addition, students may have to practice these skills on a simple level — e.g., have students work with one other student rather than in groups of five.

— Small group instruction may frequently be needed in a classroom of students with diverse achievement levels. Students should be carefully assessed on specific skills in order to form short term skill groups. It is important to keep assessing and reforming groups as necessary.

When Planning the Signal for Attention
(Also see appendix.)

— Consider using a strong signal; e.g., ring a bell, turn off lights.

— Use fun or novel signals; e.g., play Simon Says.

— Change the signal periodically.

— Let students design the signal.

— Teach students to respond quickly to the signal. Have them practice.

— Spend time teaching and reviewing what "attention" looks like and sounds like.

— Strongly reinforce students for attending quickly.

— Help students be prepared for the signal at the beginning of lessons or activities by having the daily schedule written on the board; by listing the materials needed for the next lesson/activity; and by providing reminders; e.g., "In five minutes we'll be starting math."

When Planning Behavior Expectations
(Also see appendix.)

— Be absolutely clear and specific. Say "Eyes on

me, mouth closed, hands on desk, listen" rather that "Pay attention while I read the story."

— Consider using visual aids; e.g., using a green flag to mean "Talking is okay."

— Make sure expectations are realistic and important for learning. Decisions should be based on students' needs, not on the teacher's personal preferences. The goal should not be a classroom in which students never talk nor move. However, students may learn best in a quiet, orderly, structured environment.

— Be brief; do not ramble.

— Be consistent in language; i.e., the same terms and phrases should be used as when the rule, procedure, or expectation was originally taught.

— Evaluate whether you need to reteach lessons on asking for help, making transitions, or other instructional routines.

— Evaluate whether you need to develop more efficient routines and procedures.

— If students are not meeting expectations, evaluate the lesson or activity for difficulty level, pacing, clarity, and other areas. Look carefully at seatwork and small group work.

— Write a specific behavior management plan for what will be done when students meet or do not meet behavior expectations. Involve students in this planning. Use strong and immediate reinforcers.

When Planning the Opening

— Add drama, humor, novelty, or excitement in order to gain attention; e.g., use skits, puppets, music, video clips, jokes, riddles, or demonstrations.

— Personalize by using the students' names and experiences; e.g., open a writing lesson with a sentence, or a math lesson with a word problem, about the students. ("If Mrs. Donahue's champion third graders win 16 games of four square...")

— Involve those students in the opening who are the most difficult to motivate or focus.

— Increase time spent on the review of earlier lessons or prerequisite skills and knowledge. Carefully plan ongoing daily, weekly, and monthly reviews.

— Involve everyone in active responses; e.g., have all students write the definition of a term from yesterday's lesson rather than asking "Who remembers what ratio means?" and then calling on a volunteer.

— Invite students to write or to say everything they already know about a topic in three minutes.

— Use the opening to build up background knowledge. For example, if students will be reading a story which takes place on a subway and they have no experience with subways, preteach necessary information.

— Computer software is available which can help develop graphic organizers to show students connections in learning or to preview lessons.

When Planning the Lesson Body or Activity Middle

Providing Directions, Procedures, Rules

1. Shorten and simplify.

2. Cue with numbers; e.g., first, second.

3. Present orally and in writing; use picture directions; provide demonstrations of what students are to do.

4. Follow up by asking questions or by having students repeat or paraphrase what they are to do.

5. Emphasize key words with intonations in your voice or by highlighting in written directions.

Presenting Information

1. Repeat key ideas often, using the same wording.

2. Ask for frequent active responses; e.g., have children process, verbally or in writing, information just presented. Decrease the use of strategies which involve calling on a few students who raise hands or asking several students to come up to the board and do a problem. Increase opportunities for all students to respond.

3. Break up the information. Teach a couple of steps, have students practice, teach a couple more, and so on. But, keep reminding students of the whole task or big picture through demonstrations or by using graphic organizers, etc.

4. Use analogies, metaphors, vivid language.

5. Be sure examples used are familiar to the students.

6. Increase use of visual aids, such as photographs, videos, real objects, and computer multimedia presentations.

7. Cue note-taking; e.g., "first," "second;" "this is important."

8. Provide partially filled-in note taking guides or *graphic organizers* which students can complete; e.g., outlines, concept maps, webs.

9. Stop often to summarize, review, and clarify how this information fits into the larger picture.

10. Provide mnemonic devices to help students remember information.

11. Adjust pacing — a brisker pace typically helps students attend and allows more teaching.

Questioning

1. If students are allowed to call out answers rather than required to raise hands, keep track of (or ask someone else to keep track of) whom is responding. If some students are consistently left out, rethink the use of this method.

2. Avoid calling only on the same few students who raise their hands quickly. Increase wait time. Develop a system for keeping track of whom you have called on; e.g., use seating chart, name sticks.

3. It is usually most effective to ask a question, pause, then call on a student by name, rather than saying, "Ben, what is the definition of...?" This encourages all students to be thinking of the definition, not just Ben. However, sometimes saying the name first may increase the involvement and success of particular students.

4. Call on nonvolunteers more often. Draw name cards at random or deliberately choose certain students to answer particular questions. The intention is *not* to embarrass students. Tell the class in advance that you will be calling on nonvolunteers and allow them to "pass" if they choose. The purpose is to keep all students attentive and to send the message that you want to hear from everyone — even those in the back row!

5. Ask frequent questions and use *active participation* strategies to get responses from all students. Make sure these strategies are varied. Make sure everyone really is participating during unison and signaled responses. Plan how to regain attention — e.g., after working with partner — or how to have

students show they are ready to go on — e.g., look at you, put pencil down.

6. Questions can be used to keep students focused while they are listening/watching. For example, hand out a list of questions before the lecture/speech, video, or story/reading. Each student takes notes on the questions during the presentation. Divide the class into teams. Give each team time to go over the questions together, to write and compare responses, and to help each other learn the material. Make name cards for each team member. Alternately pick a name card, at random, from each team's stack and call on that person to answer a question from the list. Team members cannot help each other at this point. Keep track of each team's correct answers. Teams which answer the questions correctly may be excused from the homework assignment.

Demonstrating

1. Increase the number of demonstrations.

2. Emphasize/highlight important parts or steps in demonstrations.

3. When demonstrating self-talk and self-questioning, be sure to use consistent terms and phrasing.

4. Point to steps on a written list as they are demonstrated.

5. Use videotaped demonstrations showing in-context applications, various actors, etc.

6. In addition to showing a completed product, show partially completed products along the way.

Providing Supervised Practice

1. Increase the amount of initial practice with teacher support; e.g., "Say it with me." "Do it with me."

2. Provide more structure and cues at first; e.g., an outline of a letter showing where to write the date, the greeting, and the other parts.

3. Use similar examples for initial practice. Gradually change.

4. Provide error drill.

5. Increase the amount of initial practice with peer support by using more partner or small group situations.

6. Structure small group and partner practice by teaching students how to work together. (See Chapter 11.)

7. Increase the amount of individual supervised practice with immediate feedback.

8. Build high levels of accuracy and fluency.

When Planning Extended Practice

— Build in frequent review of basic skills; e.g., at beginning of lessons, during end of day activities, in learning centers.

— Reduce length of each practice session but provide more practice sessions.

— To avoid boredom during a practice session, change the task without changing the content; e.g., tell students to 'say' an answer versus 'write' an answer; or to write answer on paper, on the blackboard, on a transparency; or to use computer practice programs.

— Make it fun — use a game format.

— Increase amount of support during practice; e.g., study guides; peer tutors; visual aids, such as posters; desktop number lines.

— When possible, provide practice in context as part of real tasks.

— When using homework, go over directions and begin during class. Be sure the task is the same or similar to supervised practice. (Salend and Gajria, 1995)

When Planning the Closing

— Do not assume that students will automatically apply or generalize the new skill or knowledge. Be very direct about where and when to use it.

— Actively involve students in summarizing at the end of the activity or lesson.

— Use the closing as one more practice opportunity.

When Planning for Evaluation
(Also see "When Planning the Objective.")

— Be sure you have taught what you are testing.

— Keep the form of evaluation as direct and simple as possible so that you are not inadvertently testing skills irrelevant to the objective; e.g., testing reading skills in math word problems.

— Keep evaluating for retention and for improvement.

When Planning for Classroom Management

— Think about the planned lesson/activity. Has everything possible been done to make it interesting and motivating? Are students likely to be involved and successful? Effective instruction helps prevent behavior problems.

— Think about the room arrangement as related to the planned activity/lesson. Will students be able to see you, the blackboard, the poster, or whatever is necessary? Will you be able to see and get close to all students? Are desks/tables set up for class discussions, small group work, individual work? Who is sitting by whom? Who is sitting near you?

— Think about the transitions within the activity/lesson. Are directions planned for moving from desks to sitting on the rug; for moving chairs together for partner work; or for switching from large group presentation to individual seatwork?

— Plan for the efficient use of time. This will also help prevent behavior problems. For example, think about needed materials and equipment. Does the VCR work? Are pens for writing on the whiteboard available? Are the copies of the handout ready? Is an efficient way to distribute materials planned? When will they be distributed so they are not a distraction? Are directions planned for how and how not to use them? Has safety been planned for? Are there directions for how to share materials and how to return them? (One of our practicum students wrote in her journal that she needed more practice in planning activities that involved the use of glue.)

— Plan how and when students will be reminded of the various routines they have been taught which relate to this activity or lesson; e.g., where to turn in assignments; how to get help; what to do when finished; how to set up for partner practice.

— Many of the strategies listed under "When Planning the Lesson Body or Activity Middle" apply to the above content; e.g., give directions verbally, in writing, with pictures, through demonstrations.

— Examine the plan and note those places where students may have difficulties; e.g., staying on task at learning centers. Plan how to provide needed structure and support to avoid problems; e.g., assign specific tasks to complete, provide use of peer helpers, etc.

— Use stronger reinforcers; e.g., use activity reinforcers in addition to praise.

— Be sure the reinforcers chosen are actually reinforcing to the students. Involve them in the selection and provide a menu of reinforcers from which to choose.

— Clarify contingencies. Be very specific — for example, do not say "If everyone tries hard..."

— Use immediate reinforcers; not a popcorn party a week away.

— Plan negative consequences for inappropriate behavior and make sure students are aware of them. Be fair and consistent, not arbitrary. Interrupt the activity or lesson as little as possible.

— Look once again at your *statement of behavior expectations*. Communicating expectations very clearly is an important way to prevent management problems.

When Planning for the Provision of Materials and Equipment

— Provide materials which support students; e.g., study guides, note taking guides, graphic organizers, highlighted texts, taped materials.

— Highlight key words or features on worksheets and put less material on each page.

— Include self-correcting materials and software, programmed materials, calculators, video and audio tape recorders — each can be very useful in helping students work independently.

— Provide students with laptop computers for note taking and/or for doing assignments, along with software for checking spelling and grammar, for word prediction, and so on.

PART 2
DIVERSITY STRATEGIES
BY PROBLEM OR DIFFICULTY

As you are planning, you are not only thinking about the various components of your lessons and activities and how to make them most effective, you are also thinking specifically about your students. You may be thinking — "There's a long

list of steps to follow in this lesson, and my class has trouble with that. What can I do to help them be successful?" Or you may be thinking — "Tim, Andrew, Bridget, and Anne are going to have a hard time sitting down long enough to finish this assignment. How can I help them?" The following strategies may be built into the initial planning for the whole class or used as accommodations for individuals. (Cohen and Lynch, 1991) Many of the ideas come from the literature on instructional recommendations for students with attention deficits but will be helpful for many students (Bender and Mathes, 1995; Council for Exceptional Children, 1992; Kemp, Fister, and McLaughlin, 1995; Lerner, Lowenthal, and Lerner, 1995; Rooney, 1995; Yehle and Wambold, 1998).

Planning for Students
Who Have Difficulty With

- ☐ keeping still
- ☐ waiting
- ☐ selective attention
- ☐ maintaining attention
- ☐ routine tasks
- ☐ memorizing
- ☐ beginning tasks
- ☐ completing tasks
- ☐ following directions
- ☐ organizing
- ☐ reading
- ☐ handwriting
- ☐ messiness
- ☐ taking tests
- ☐ change
- ☐ self control

Difficulty Keeping Still

— Let student stand or move when this isn't disruptive to learning; e.g. stand at desk to do independent work, walk around while doing oral practice.

— Allow student to use various desks or work areas.

— Let student use worry beads or doodle when this does not interfere with the task.

— Build in movement for students in the daily schedule; e.g., hand out papers, run errands, clean up, do stretching exercises.

— Build in movement in lessons and activities by using active physical responses; e.g., tell students to "stand up if you think this is the topic sentence" or "walk to the blackboard and write the definition."

— Teach students to signal when needing a break.

Difficulty Waiting/Impulsiveness
(When in line, when taking turns, in responding on assignments or tests, during discussions, etc.)

— Use wait time after questions and do not allow call-outs.

— Tell students to discuss response with their partner before saying or writing the answer.

— Teach student to underline/highlight important words in test questions or in assignment directions.

— Cue the use of problem-solving steps.

— Teach student to outline essay test answers before writing.

— Teach student to think of the answer on his/her own before looking at multiple choices on a test.

— Teach student what to do while waiting for help; e.g., try another problem or task; ask a partner for help; read a book.

— Cue the use of self-talk; e.g., "I need to take a deep breath and..."

— Provide student with something to do while waiting in line or for a turn; e.g., play a game, sing a song, have something in the pocket to play with.

— Teach student how to interrupt politely; e.g., touch, recognize pauses.

Difficulty with Selective Attention
(i.e., attending to the important aspects of a task or information.) (See Howell, Fox, and Morehead, 1993, Chapter 17 for suggestions to promote attention, memory, and motivation.)

— Use color cues, highlight, or bold important details.

— Provide study guides and other comprehension supports — such as advance questions — to go with readings or presentations.

— Provide flash cards or cue cards which include key information and examples with no extraneous information.

— Use a consistent format for instruction and on worksheets.

Difficulty Maintaining Attention

— Provide preferential seating; e.g., sit near teacher or other adult; sit near quiet peers; sit away from high traffic areas, doors, windows; sit at individual desk rather than at table with other students.

— Reduce distractions in the short run, but teach student to ignore distractions in the long run; e.g., through preferential seating; through use of study carrels, screens, or headphones; by reduced sounds and visual stimuli.

— Provide more frequent breaks or changes in task.

— Use more *active participation* strategies.

51

— Regain student's attention frequently through proximity, touch, eye contact, private signals.

— Teach student to self monitor attention/on task (Kaplan, 1995, Chapter 9).

— Have peer helper prompt student to pay attention.

Difficulty Sticking with Routine Tasks

— Divide task into smaller segments, with brief break or reinforcement between segments, or spread task throughout the day/class.

— Remove anything unnecessary from task; e.g., copying sentence before correcting it.

— Analyze the amount of practice needed — remove unnecessary repetitions; make sure difficulty level is appropriate; and make sure the objective is important.

— Alternate tasks so that tasks which student prefers follow the less preferred ones.

— Alternate forms of practice; e.g., to practice math problems — write on paper, write on board, work with partner.

— Add novelty/interest; e.g., with games, materials, personal interests.

— Teach on-task behavior, including self-monitoring and self-reinforcement.

Difficulty with Tasks That Require Memory

— Incorporate (and teach) memory strategies, such as mnemonics, visualizing, oral practice or rehearsal, many repetitions — e.g., teach students to make a word or sentence using first letters of words in a list to be learned or help students memorize new terms using picture clues and known words (Mastropieri and Scruggs, 1998).

Difficulty Beginning Tasks

— Provide cue card on desk, describing how to begin a task. Have student check off steps as completed; e.g., (1) Write name on paper, (2) Read directions, etc. (This is similar to reminders on billing envelopes, such as "Have you written the account number on the check?")

— Go to student quickly at the start of seatwork. Help him/her start. Say that you will be back shortly to check.

— Provide peer helper to prompt or to do first step/problem together.

Difficulty Completing Tasks

— Assist student to set goal for task completion within realistic time limits and self-reinforce.

— Clarify what constitutes completion; e.g., answer all five questions in complete sentences; put name on paper; place paper in assignment box on teacher's desk. Write this on board or on cue card on student's desk.

— Establish routines for turning in assignments; e.g., determine where and when.

— Provide peer help in reminding to finish tasks and turn them in.

— Help student list tasks to do and check them off as completed.

Difficulty Following Directions

— Before giving directions, make sure you have the student's attention; e.g., gain eye contact, say name, touch.

— Give only one or two directions at a time.

— Simplify the language and vocabulary.

— Emphasize key words.

— Ask the student to repeat the directions — at first to you and eventually to self.

— Give students their own copy of written directions.

— Have a peer read directions to the student.

— Teach the student to circle important words in written directions.

— Teach and follow consistent routines so directions do not have to be given too often.

Difficulty Organizing

— List assignments and materials needed on board or transparency.

— Teach student to use an assignment calendar, a checklist, etc.

— Have students use notebooks with pockets or dividers.

— Provide places to put materials on desk or in room; e.g. in boxes, on trays.

— Help students color code materials needed for various subjects.

— Provide time to gather materials or books at beginning/end of class/day.

— Teach a consistent routine for turning in or picking up assignments.

— Provide peer help.

— Help student divide tasks into steps or parts.

Difficulty Reading
(When reading instruction or practice is not the objective.)

— Have a peer or other volunteer read to the student.

— Have a peer summarize information orally to the student.

— Provide highlighted text.

— Provide study guides, outlines, or graphic organizers to go with the reading in order to help with comprehension.

— Provide the necessary information in other forms, such as oral presentations, audio tapes, video tapes, or computer multimedia programs.

Slow and/or Poor Handwriting

— Teach handwriting and provide for increased practice to build fluency. Provide practice using content of personal interest; e.g., copy information about music groups.

— Give student a copy of your notes or a copy of peer's notes.

— When the objective of the lesson or activity is *not* to teach/practice handwriting, consider the following:

- decrease nonessential writing; e.g., do not require student to copy question before writing answer.
- allow use of other methods — such as using a word processor, giving oral presentations, having someone take dictation, taping answers.
- do not worry as long as it is readable.

Messiness

— Allow student to use pencil and eraser; to use graph paper, which helps organize writing on a page; or to use a word processor.

— Provide time and support for cleaning desk or work area.

— Provide places and reminders of where to put things; e.g., in boxes, on shelves, in an extra desk, in notebooks.

Difficulty with Taking Tests

— Allow alternative forms of testing; e.g., oral rather than written.

— Provide help with understanding directions for taking tests.

— Teach test-taking skills; e.g., cross out incorrect answers on multiple choice tests; outline answers on essay tests.

Difficulty with Change
(Some students become upset at changes in schedule and routines or in having different people in the classroom, etc.)

— Maintain the same schedule of events, as much as possible, in the classroom. Post and discuss the schedule.

— Warn student of changes in advance; e.g., an assembly this afternoon; a parent visitor.

— Support student through the change; e.g., have him stay near you or a designated peer; give reminders of expected behavior; provide words of comfort.

— Remind student to use previously taught relaxation techniques.

— Initially provide practice in dealing with change through role plays and controlled minor changes.

Difficulty with Behavioral Self Control
(Kaplan, 1995; Rhode, Jenson, and Reavis, 1993)

— Be sure lessons and activities are appropriate for student.

— Teach self-management and social skills — such as problem solving, anger management, stress management.

— Use precorrection plans (Walker, Colvin, and Ramsey, 1995, Chapter 7).

— Be observant and intervene early.

— Provide structure and consistency.

— Spend time developing a warm, personal relationship with student.

— Keep student busy; e.g., with entry tasks; with tasks to do when finished with assignment or while waiting for help; during brief transitions.

— Carefully teach and provide practice on rules, procedures, and class routines.

— Develop a written behavior management plan that is clear and that includes positive and negative consequences.

— Seat student near you or selected peers.

— Arrange a time-out area.

— Use strong, frequent, immediate reinforcers.

— Use behavior contracts.

— Use novel reinforcement systems.

— Involve parents.

— Use peer mediation.

Note: There are many, many more diversity strategies described in the professional literature. See the end of the chapter for suggested readings.

PART 3
PLANNING FOR CULTURAL DIVERSITY

Cultural diversity needs to be considered when planning lessons and activities. It is important to be educated about cultures and cultural perspectives. It is also important to be aware of your own cultural background and how this affects beliefs, values, expectations and, in turn, the choice of subject matter, models, methods, management procedures, rules, and so on. There must be an awareness about the particular cultures of the students and how these affect the students' preferences and reactions to the methods and management used in the classroom. However, it is extremely important to see students first as individuals. The importance of cultural background must be recognized, but it is essential to avoid stereotyping. Think of the purpose of understanding cultural diversity as that of making you a better decision maker or problem solver; i.e., being able to generate more ideas or options when planning.

When planning, consider two general areas in which to provide for cultural diversity: *content* and *instruction/management*. (Cartledge and Milburn, 1995, Chapter 10; Grossman, 1991; Grossman, 1995; Manning and Baruth, 1996). When planning content, incorporate subject matter, materials, and examples which reflect the contributions and perspectives of a variety of cultures and the personal experiences and interests of the students. The purpose is to help all of the students feel valued, represented, and motivated and to help the students become knowledgeable and tolerant (or, more importantly, welcoming) of diversity.

In the selection of models and methods of instruction and management, consider the possible cultural preferences and experiences of the students. There is a real danger of stereotyping or overgeneralizing here; e.g., thinking that all African-American students learn best through cooperative learning. To avoid this, make a best guess as to which methods will work most successfully for particular students and then monitor their progress carefully, changing methods as needed. Since all students are not the same, a variety of models and methods should be used when planning activities and lessons for the whole class, as well as individualizing for particular students.

Planning the Content

Long-Range Planning

There should be a multicultural perspective throughout the curriculum as well as specific units of instruction with multicultural content.

The content of daily lessons and activities will be based on these larger perspectives and units of instruction. Even though long-range planning is beyond the scope of this book, it is important to mention that there are many options for bringing a multicultural focus to the content of units; e.g., units on the contributions of particular cultural groups; units on topics such as the history of the civil rights movement and immigration; and units on themes such as conflict resolution, social justice, and stereotyping.

Daily Planning

A multicultural focus to activities and lessons which are not part of units on multicultural topics may also be included. For example, to provide practice on distinguishing between main ideas and details (the objective), a story is read to students. They are to brainstorm a list of what they remember from the story and then sort main ideas and details (the activity). Since the topic of the story is irrelevant to the objective, a story could be selected for a "cultural" purpose; e.g., a story about an individual with a disability, one about a homeless family, or an African folk tale. The "cultural" purpose may be to help individual students feel that their experiences or backgrounds are represented and valued in the classroom or to provide information about experiences or cultures unfamiliar to the students.

Another example might be the selection of an art activity to provide practice on the long-term objective of following directions. An art form of a particular culture could be selected. There are many activities — especially in reading, writing, art, and music — where cultural information may be incorporated as an additional goal.

The same holds true for the selection of "carrier" content in lessons. For example, a teacher is planning a lesson with the objective that students will identify nouns in sentences. Some students come from families who fish for a living and where fishing is an important aspect of their culture. The sentences used as examples or during practice could be about fishing. However, be very careful to avoid stereotyping with this technique; e.g., including sentences about sombreros or tepees.

It is also important to consider cultural diversity when planning activities and lessons on topics — such as Thanksgiving, Columbus Day, and Mother's Day — in order to ensure that various perspectives or "voices" are represented. Be sensitive to diversity when planning assignments — for example, designing a family tree, writing letters to Santa — and when planning social skills lessons — for example, teaching assertiveness.

Note: Teachers need to send a message of welcome and respect by learning the correct pronunciation and use of names. They should also learn the languages of their students (at least hello, goodbye, thank you, etc.), encourage the use of native languages, and include pictures and other materials which represent various cultures. Materials used in the classroom should reflect cultural diversity and must be examined to make sure they are free of bias.

Planning Instruction and Management

Cultural background can influence students' success with particular instructional and management methods. It is essential to see students as individuals and to make individual decisions, but knowledge of how culture contributes to variation can be helpful in thinking of instruction and management possibilities. For example, if a teacher has a student who does not ask for help on assignments when he needs it, knowledge of his cultural background may suggest trying a same-sex peer helper. The teacher must carefully monitor for the effectiveness of this strategy and be ready to try other methods if needed. However, this may be a sensible first try.

To avoid stereotyping, we have not categorized ideas by cultural group but, instead, have listed *variables or possibilities to consider* as you plan for instruction and for management (Grossman, 1991).

Instruction

The success of instruction is dependent on how well individual needs of students are met.

Consider your students':

1. preference for learning from peers or from adults.

2. comfort with competition or cooperation.

3. preference for individual or group work.

4. valuing of generosity and sharing — implications for helping each other on assignments, even tests.

5. expectations about interactions with the opposite sex; e.g., there may be problems with having a boy and girl as learning partners.

6. beliefs about excelling or standing out from peers.

Think about the students in terms of the above variables as the use of peer interactive instruction and practice is considered. You may wish to try, for example, increasing or decreasing the amount of partner practice or the use of peer tutoring and various cooperative learning methods. You may consider these variables as decisions are made about the composition of groups and student roles, about using competitive game formats, and about publicly displaying accomplishments. Also, consider that one of the goals of using peer groups may be to promote cross cultural interaction and friendships and to discourage segregation by race, social class, etc.

Consider your students':

7. comfort with making their own decisions, initiating their own projects, and choosing what or how to learn.

8. tolerance for structure or lack of structure.

9. experience with sitting quietly or with maintaining high activity levels.

10. comfort with the teacher as a co-learner or as an authority.

11. desire for feedback, direction.

12. independence or dependence on teacher.

13. beliefs about asking for help or questioning the teacher.

The variables above have implications for the selection of lesson models and the use or structuring of project or center based activities. As activities and lessons are planned, think about the teacher's role, the pacing of instruction, the amount of talk and movement, the specificity of directions, and other features.

Consider your students':

14. comfort with stating opinions, stating opinions passionately, disagreeing with others — including the teacher.

15. comfort with volunteering to answer questions; initiating their own questions or comments.

16. experience with divergent or open-ended questions.

17. beliefs as to what constitutes polite responses to questions or statements; methods of interrupting.

18. beliefs about how much talking is polite.

Think about the above variables as you plan discussions and brainstorming sessions, active participation strategies, and questioning techniques; e.g., calling on volunteers and nonvolunteers.

Consider your students':

19. differences in prior knowledge and personal experience; e.g., ask yourself if you are assuming a familiarity with St. Patrick's Day, dairy farms, escalators, and other topics, as you plan activities and lessons.

Consider the above variable when you are planning topics, selecting readings, and planning openings.

Consider your students':

20. proficiency with the English language.

If you are teaching in English and students have limited proficiency with the language, provide information in verbal and written form; use concrete objects, pictures, videos, and demonstrations; include repetition and active participation. Peer partners and small groups can be helpful in communication practice. Provide support by peers with the same native language. As you are considering what key terms and vocabulary to teach in a lesson, remember the difference between social language and academic language proficiency.

Management

Responses to management techniques may also be influenced by cultural background.

Consider your students':

1. expectations about relationships with adults having to do with respect, showing affection, and gender issues.

2. preferences for close, warm, informal relationships or more distant, formal relationships with teachers.

3. preferences about touching and being touched.

4. beliefs about talking and conversations — considering the amount, who initiates, sharing personal information, and what is considered private.

5. expectations about relationships with peers — considering age and gender issues, extended family, teasing, fighting, sharing, excelling.

6. differences in nonverbal communication — including the communication of motivation, interest, listening.

Think about the above variables when analyzing your interactions with students and when evaluating the social climate in the classroom. Do not assume your students are just like you. They may be horrified if you sit on the floor with them or ask them to call you by your first name. They may believe you do not like them if you do not hug them or ask about their families. Do not make assumptions that you all agree on what is polite or respectful behavior.

Consider your students':

7. expectations about rules and procedures — who develops them, what are they, what level of strictness.

8. beliefs about obedience, about adult authority, about arguing with or questioning adults, about providing rationale for rules or decisions.

9. need for structure and organization, for a quiet environment, for clear goals and expectations.

10. value of conformity.

11. expectations about asking permission or about functioning independently; e.g., borrowing materials, going to the restroom.

12. changes in expectations by age or gender.

The above variables have clear implications for the development of classroom rules and procedures and for the behavior expectations component of activities and lessons.

Consider your students':

13. comfort with public or private recognition and punishment.

14. comfort with individual versus group acknowledgment or reinforcement.

15. preference for personal reinforcement, such as warm praise, rather than more impersonal reinforcement, such as prizes.

16. value of praise or criticism from others — such as from peers or teacher.

17. familiarity with different types of punishment; e.g., shaming, corporal, discussions.

The above variables will clearly affect the planning of behavior consequences. Do not assume what will be reinforcing or punishing to individual students.

Since each student is unique, the instructional and management methods and the decisions for individuals need to be varied. In some instances, students may need to be taught to become comfortable with approaches that they are not used to. In other cases, the teacher will need to adjust to the fact that certain behaviors are impermissible for some students for cultural or religious reasons.

We have suggested only a few of the many variations possible among cultures. You can see how important it is to become knowledgeable about cultural diversity in general and your own and your students' cultural backgrounds in particular.

SUMMARY

The students you work with will be diverse in their success with various teaching and management methods. The key to planning is to make decisions based on the students' needs rather than your own preferences. The suggestions presented in this chapter are only a beginning. It is important to continue to add to your repertoire of diversity strategies.

* * * * * * * * * * * * * * * * * * * *

REFERENCES AND SUGGESTED READINGS

Algozzine, B., and J. Ysseldyke. *Strategies and Tactics for Effective Instruction*. Longmont, CO: Sopris West, 1992.

Bender, W.N., and M.Y. Mathes. "Students with ADHD in the Inclusive Classroom: A Hierarchical Approach to Strategy Selection." *Intervention in School and Clinic, 30.* pp. 226-234. 1995.

Cartledge, G., and J. Milburn. *Teaching Social Skills to Children and Youth*. Needham Heights, MA: Allyn and Bacon, 1995.

Cegelka, P.T., and W.H. Berdine. *Effective Instruction for Students with Learning Difficulties*. Needham Heights, MA: Allyn and Bacon, 1995.

Cohen, S.B., and D.K. Lynch. "An Instructional Modification Process." *Teaching Exceptional Children, 23.* pp. 12-18. 1991.

Council for Exceptional Children. *Children with ADD: A Shared Responsibility*. Reston, VA: Author, 1992.

Cummings, C. *Teaching Makes a Difference*. 2nd ed. Edmonds, WA: Teaching, Inc., 1990.

Evertson, C.M., E.T. Emmer, B.S. Clements, and M.E. Worsham. *Classroom Management for Elementary Teachers*. 3rd ed. Needham Heights, MA: Allyn and Bacon, 1994.

Fisher, J.B., J.B. Schumaker, and D.D. Deshler. "Searching for Validated Inclusive Practices: A Review of the Literature." *Focus on Exceptional Children, 28.* pp. 1-20. 1995.

Grossman, H. "Multicultural Classroom Management." *Contemporary Education, 62.* pp. 161-166. 1991.

Grossman, H. *Classroom Behavior Management in a Diverse Society*. 2nd ed. Mountain View, CA: Mayfield, 1995.

Howell, K.W., S.L. Fox, and M.K. Morehead. *Curriculum-Based Evaluation: Teaching and Decision Making.* 2nd ed. Pacific Grove, CA: Brooks/Cole, 1993.

Kaplan, J.S. *Beyond Behavior Modification.* 3rd ed. Austin, TX: Pro-Ed, 1995.

Kemp, K., S. Fister, and P.J. McLaughlin. "Academic Strategies for Children with ADD." *Intervention in School and Clinic, 30.* pp. 203-210. 1995.

Lerner, J.W., B. Lowenthal, and S.R. Lerner. *Attention Deficit Disorders.* Pacific Grove, CA: Brooks/Cole, 1995.

Lovitt, T.C. *Tactics for Teaching.* 2nd ed. Englewood Cliffs, NJ: Prentice Hall, 1995.

Manning, M.L., and L.G. Baruth. *Multicultural Education of Children and Adolescents.* 2nd ed. Needham Heights, MA: Allyn and Bacon, 1996.

Mastropieri, M.A., and T.E. Scruggs. "Enhancing School Success with Mnemonic Strategies." *Intervention in School and Clinic, 33.* pp. 201-208. 1998.

Meltzer, L.J., B.N. Roditi, D.P. Haynes, K.R. Biddle, M. Paster, and S.E. Taber. *Strategies for Success: Classroom Teaching Techniques for Students with Learning Problems.* Austin, TX: Pro-Ed., 1996.

Prater, M.A. "Increasing Time on Task in the Classroom." *Intervention in School and Clinic, 28.* pp. 22-27. 1992.

Rhode, G., W. Jenson, and H. Reavis. *The Tough Kid Book.* Longmont, CO: Sopris West, 1993.

Rooney, K.J. "Teaching Students with Attention Disorders." *Intervention in School and Clinic, 30.* pp. 221-225. 1995.

Salend, S.J., and M. Gajria. "Increasing the Homework Completion Rates of Students with Mild Disabilities." *Remedial and Special Education, 16.* pp. 271-278. 1995.

Sprick, R., M. Sprick, and M. Garrison. *Interventions: Collaborative Planning for Students at Risk.* Longmont, CO: Sopris West, 1993.

Walker, H., G. Colvin, and E. Ramsey. *Antisocial Behavior in School: Strategies and Best Practices.* Pacific Grove, CA: Brooks/Cole, 1995.

Yehle, A.K., and C. Wambold. "An ADHD Success Story: Strategies for Teachers and Students." *Teaching Exceptional Children, 30.* pp. 8-13. 1998.

Preface
to the
Lesson Models

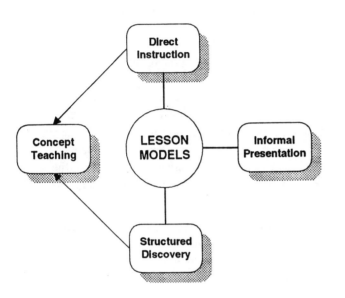

INTRODUCTION

A lesson model is an overall teaching approach that is used to guide student learning in a specific way toward the attainment of a lesson objective (Arends, 1997, pg. 7). There are various lesson models for which lesson plans are written. In Chapters 7, 8, and 9, there is information about three important lesson models. These are direct instruction, informal presentation, and structured discovery. Chapter 10 presents information on how to use two of these models to teach concepts.

These three models were included in this book because they are reasonably easy for beginning teachers to implement, and they are very effective when used correctly. Additionally, they can be used to facilitate different types of learning.

A beginning teacher needs to be able to successfully implement these three lesson models.

Using various models and methods is essential because variety helps keep students motivated and interested; variety addresses the fact that not all students learn in the same way; and certain content is best taught through certain models. It is also important to incorporate the use of peers into lessons and activities. This topic is covered in Chapter 11.

One model might be practiced several times until you are comfortable with it; then start practicing another model. A practicum student and/or student teacher has the opportunity to practice writing and teaching single lessons before being expected to teach multiple lessons within one day. This allows time to experiment with and practice teaching various lesson models.

SELECTING A MODEL TO USE

Students are guided toward a specific lesson objective in different ways, depending on the lesson model used. Some models work well for teaching basic knowledge and skills; e.g., direct instruction and informal presentation. Some models may be used to promote inductive thinking and problem-solving skills; e.g., structured discovery and concept teaching. Therefore, a thorough understanding of the characteristics of various lesson models can help determine which particular model would best benefit the students so that a particular objective could be mastered.

A lesson model should always be selected after the lesson objective(s) is written — decide first where you want students to go (i.e., the lesson objective) and *then* decide how to help get them there (i.e., the lesson model). Once the model to use in the lesson is selected, it is necessary to be sure the written plan reflects the essential elements of the chosen model. For example, if you are writing a direct instruction lesson, the plan should detail how you will explain and demonstrate information; how you will check for understanding; and what types of practice opportunities will be provided. These are key elements of a direct instruction lesson. Although all lesson plans contain the same eight components, the content of the components will differ depending on the lesson model being used.

ORGANIZATION OF CHAPTERS 7-10

Similar information about direct instruction, informal presentation, and structured discovery models is presented. A basic model description introduces each model. Next, typical uses for the model are described. Some key elements of each model are discussed in "Key Planning Considerations." Finally summaries of how to write the actual lesson plans are presented in Figures 7.1-10.1.

Concept teaching is presented in a different way. This is because concept teaching is not a lesson model in and of itself. Concepts are taught using either a structured discovery or a direct instruction model. Therefore, the emphasis in Chapter 10, "Concept Teaching - A Special Case," is the actual content to be taught (i.e., concepts) rather than *how* to teach them.

Figures 7.1-10.1 are to be used as guides for writing lesson plans for specific lesson models. They are, in fact, summaries. Our intent is for you to read carefully *all* of the information provided about each model and use it as a reference when you write your plans. The summaries can serve as reminders of the key information that needs to be included in the written plans. *Note*: Refer to Chapter 5 for information about generic lesson components.

The content of each component included in each specific model is essential to defining the model. Certain component content may be added, rearranged, or omitted. However, if that is done, it is necessary to have a good rationale for doing so. Too much variation from the critical elements of the model will result in something other than the model which was chosen to be used. Changes must be carefully analyzed.

Note: Before selecting a specific lesson model to use, the following preplanning tasks must be completed first:

▸ Determine the specific content to be taught in the lesson and analyze that content.

▸ Write the lesson objective.

▸ Write the lesson rationale.

▸ NOW, select the model and refer to the appropriate chapter for more information.

Chapter 7

Direct Instruction

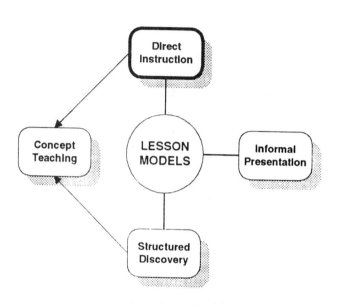

INTRODUCTION

Direct instruction is often summarized as "I do it, We do it, You do it" — that is, the teacher demonstrates the skill, the teacher and students do the skill together, the students do the skill by themselves. Another phrase used to describe direct instruction is "model-lead-test." It means the teacher shows/tells, the teacher leads the students in practicing, and the students are evaluated. Both phrases imply that the teacher is carefully guiding the learning of the students. This is precisely the intent of direct instruction. Direct instruction is *explicit* teaching.

Direct instruction lessons are teacher directed, and the lesson events are focused on moving students toward a specific objective. The teacher begins by clearly stating the lesson objective and the lesson purpose to the students. She/he then explains and demonstrates the information or skill to be learned,

using many examples. Students are given a variety of opportunities to practice the new knowledge or skill. The teacher carefully supervises the students' practice, which may occur within small groups or with a partner. The final supervised practice stage is always individual student practice. This allows the teacher to see how *each* student is progressing.

Students are given feedback on their performance as the teacher monitors the supervised practice opportunities. This helps ensure that students are accurately practicing the new information or skill. Careful monitoring also allows the teacher to determine whether or not reteaching is needed and when evaluation should occur.

A direct instruction approach presents information in small steps so that one step can be mastered before moving to the next. The end result of the direct instruction lesson is that students demonstrate their new skill or knowledge independently, without help from anyone.

Note: There are two types of direct instruction. One type, often called "Big D.I.," refers to published programs which provide scripted lessons; e.g., Reading Mastery I and II Fast Cycle (Engelmann & Bruner, 1995). The other type, commonly referred to as "little d.i.," is the one described in this chapter. Both types of direct instruction are characterized by a teacher's explicit guidance of student learning toward specific objectives. The explanations, directions, and other material contained in "little d.i." lessons, however, are created by the individual writing the lesson plan.

USES OF DIRECT INSTRUCTION

Direct instruction lessons play an important role in the acquisition of basic skills and knowledge. They are appropriate for teaching basic skills, facts, concepts, strategies, procedures, and knowledge which lends itself to being presented in small, sequential steps. Some examples of content that can be appropriately taught through direction instruction lessons are the following:

▸ Basic Knowledge — parts of speech, vocabulary, parts of a research paper, the periodic table, the branches of government, the rules of soccer.

▸ Basic Skills — punctuating sentences, keyboarding, serving in volleyball, math computation, organizing and maintaining an assignment calendar, taking notes from text reading.

▸ Strategies — problem-solving steps, reading comprehension strategies, math algorithms, memorization strategies. (See the end of the chapter for suggested readings on strategy instruction.)

▸ Concepts — triangle, peninsula, noun, socialism. (See Chapter 10.)

▸ Class Rules and Procedures — displaying respect for others, correct paper headings, make-up assignments due to absence, what to do with completed work, how to get help.

▸ Social Skills — how to initiate a conversation, how to react to teasing, how to resist peer pressure.

Direct instruction lessons also play an important role in lessons which emphasize higher level thinking. Higher level thinking cannot occur without having basic facts and information about which to think. The content taught in direct instruction lessons may form the foundation for lessons which emphasize critical thinking and problem solving.

The following are some examples of how higher level thinking is dependent on knowledge of basic skills and information:

▸ Mr. Garcia wants his students to use the Internet as one resource for their country analysis. He first teaches them computer access skills through direct instruction.

▸ Ms. Sparks wants her students to design their own science experiments to test certain hypotheses. She first teaches them steps in the scientific method through direct instruction.

Direct instruction lessons also play an important role in the use of certain teaching methods (Arends, 1997). For example, if you want to use cooperative learning groups and/or discussions in your lessons and activities, students will need to be directly taught skills such as reaching consensus, taking turns, active listening, and paraphrasing.

KEY PLANNING CONSIDERATIONS

When the body of the direct instruction lesson is being written, the presentation of information, the demonstration, and the supervised practice should be carefully thought through and planned in detail.

Presentation of Information

The *presentation of information* section should include a description of what will be said to explain the new skill or knowledge. It is based on the content analysis and is a major element of the lesson body. It is important to present all of the information necessary for understanding the new knowledge or skill through explanations, descriptions, definitions, and specific examples and nonexamples. Typically the information is presented both orally and in writing. A description of the diversity strategies — e.g., graphic organizers — to be used to strengthen the presentation of information should also be included.

When the body of the lesson is written, enough detail must be included to prevent being "caught off guard" during the lesson. Do *not* simply write in the plan, "I will explain the steps" or "I'll define each term." It is necessary to plan *how* you will explain — namely, by listing in the plan the key points or ideas you want to get across. The definitions of key terms need to be written out so that they are clear and complete. It is very difficult to spontaneously explain or describe or define in a clear way. Often the ideas which seem most simple and obvious to the teacher are the most difficult to explain.

Remember that it is usually not appropriate to ask students to provide the initial explanations of the new information because it is *very* important that initial explanations are accurate and clear. Students may be involved by asking them to review prerequisite knowledge or skills *before* the presentation of information. They could also be asked for their ideas and examples *after* the necessary information has been presented.

Carefully plan how you will *check for understanding* of the information. If there is a great deal of new information, then incorporate checks for understanding and opportunities for student processing after each step or part of the information. Calling on one student to paraphrase or give an additional example will not reveal whether *all* of the students understand. Include *active participation* strategies which will allow checking everyone's understanding.

Demonstration

Before, during, or after the presentation of information, the teacher needs to demonstrate — i.e., show or model — the new knowledge or skill. The teacher may show a product (e.g., "Here is an example of a paragraph which includes a topic sentence and supporting details") and/or model a process (e.g., "Watch as I make this foul shot" or

"Listen as I think out loud while developing my topic sentence"). During the presentation of the information component, the teacher will probably show examples or demonstrate specific steps, but it is essential that she/he also models the whole product or process.

Again, it is important that the teacher provides accurate and clear demonstrations before asking students to do so. Again, it is important that the teacher creates the product or plans the *demonstration* in advance. Again, it is important that the teacher plans how to check for understanding.

Note: A common error is forgetting to teach before asking students to practice. It is essential that the teacher provides complete explanations, many examples, and many demonstrations. If you find that unnecessary, then you are most likely planning a review or practice activity rather than a direct instruction lesson. Another common error is to ask students to do the initial teaching; this is done out of eagerness to promote active participation and involvement. If students can do the initial teaching, then you most likely have planned an activity rather than a lesson. There are many ways of keeping students engaged without neglecting the responsibility of teaching clearly and accurately.

Supervised Practice

After the teacher has presented and demonstrated information, it is time to provide opportunities for the students to practice under the guidance and supervision of the teacher. (*Note:* If the new knowledge or skill is complex, the teacher may choose to provide formal *supervised practice* after each step or part.) It is very important that the teacher controls and monitors this practice so that students are not practicing errors. The teacher leads and prompts and gives corrective *feedback* immediately.

The following are three levels of supervised practice:

65

1. <u>Whole group practice</u> - The teacher may begin by demonstrating the skill again, but this time involving the class; e.g., "Let's do a problem together; what should I do first?"

2. <u>Small group or partner practice</u> - The second level involves asking students to practice with the support of peers.

3. <u>Individual practice</u> - The final and *essential* level is asking each student to practice alone while the teacher monitors and corrects.

The first two levels provide a bridge between teacher demonstration and individual practice, so that initial attempts have peer as well as teacher support.

During the presentation and demonstration section of the lesson, if the teacher checked everyone's understanding and believed they "got it," then she/he may go right to supervised *individual* practice. (*Note*: Individual supervised practice is *not* the formal evaluation.) However, if the new knowledge or skill is difficult or complex or if the teacher was not able to check everyone's understanding, then she/he will probably want to begin with whole class and/or small group or partner practice.

The practice activities must be congruent with — i.e., match — what was taught during the presentation of information and demonstration section. All parts of the lesson must be congruent with the lesson objective.

* * * * * * * * * * * * * * * * * * * *

Figure 7.1 WRITING A DIRECT INSTRUCTION LESSON

The content of the components below tells what typically would be included in each component in a direct instruction lesson plan. When you write your plan, clearly label each component — e.g., Component 1 - Preplanning Tasks — and component parts — e.g., task analysis, objective.

Component 1 - <u>PREPLANNING TASKS</u>

<u>Write</u>: (The preplanning tasks section is a cover sheet for the rest of the lesson plan.)

✎ a *content analysis* — May include a *subject matter outline, task analysis, key terms/vocabulary*, and a list of *prerequisite skills/knowledge*.

✎ an *objective* — Possible objectives for a direct instruction lesson could be for students to demonstrate, list, rewrite, give an example, identify, state reasons, label, use a strategy, compute.

✎ an *objective rationale* — To help clarify the value of the objective.

▸ Think about the flow of the lesson and remember to include diversity strategies as you plan.

Component 2 - <u>LESSON SET-UP</u>

The *lesson set-up* is the first component of the lesson plan that is actually presented to students.

<u>Write</u>:

✎ a *signal for attention* — e.g., play music, flick lights, say "Let's get started."

✎ a *statement of behavior expectations* — e.g., "If you need help, you may ask your partner."

Component 3 - LESSON OPENING

The lesson *opening* should effectively prepare the students for the new learning.

Write:

✎ a strategy designed to generate interest in the lesson and/or to relate new learning to prior knowledge.

✎ a way to *state the objective* so students know what they will learn. In a direct instruction lesson, students are told directly what they will be expected to do following the lesson.

✎ a statement of the *objective purpose* so students know why the new learning is valuable and useful.

Component 4 - LESSON BODY

The *lesson body* looks like a series of repeated steps — i.e., first, teacher "show and tell;" then, check for understanding; then, supervised practice with *feedback*; then, more teacher "show and tell;" and so on. For less complex lessons, the teacher will "show and tell" all steps and then provide supervised practice.

Write:

✎ teacher "show and tell" — The *presentation of information* and an accompanying *demonstration* that is necessary to enable the students to learn the content or perform the skill(s) being taught (or the first step in a sequence). This should include many, varied examples.

✎ techniques that will be used to *check for understanding* — These should involve overt responses on the part of the students (i.e., they do or say something) so you can determine if students are progressing toward the objective. For example, students may use thumbs up or thumbs down to signify they agree or disagree.

✎ *supervised practice* opportunities — You will *always* include individual supervised practice, but you may choose to include whole group or partner/small group practice as well. For example, you may first provide practice for the whole group (e.g., "Let's do one more problem together"). Next, students work with a partner (e.g., "You will practice the next six problems with your partner. Each of you take turns working three problems while thinking out loud, and your partner will check for accuracy.") Finally, students work alone (e.g., "Try the next two problems by yourself, and I will come around and check your answers.")

✎ the diversity strategies you will use — An important strategy to use in the direct instruction lesson is *active participation*. For example, students may compare answers with a partner, write answers on a piece of scratch paper and hold it up for you to see, or respond in unison.

Component 5 - EXTENDED PRACTICE

Extended practice is one of the key elements in the direct instruction lesson. Students will need additional practice to develop the accuracy and fluency necessary for application and generalization of the new skill or knowledge. Seatwork and homework are types of assignments that provide extended practice opportunities, and they should match the individual supervised practice in the body of the lesson. Checking these assignments carefully will let you know when formal evaluation should occur.

▸ Long-term extended practice is typically provided in the form of activities. (See Chapter 4.)

Component 5 - <u>EXTENDED PRACTICE</u> (continued)

<u>Write</u>:

- ✎ a list of additional practice opportunities, including assignments and homework, to be provided — Be sure that final practice activities provide students with an opportunity to practice alone. One diversity strategy to consider in this component is variation of extended practice opportunities. Some students will need a great deal of extended practice, while others will need far less.
- ✎ a list of lessons and activities, if appropriate, that will build on this objective and additional opportunities for students to generalize and extend the information, etc.

Component 6 - <u>LESSON CLOSING</u>

The lesson *closing* in a direct instruction lesson will occur in one of two places, following supervised practice. If extended practice is assigned as in-class work, the teacher may close the lesson after the assignment has been completed. Whereas if extended practice is assigned as homework, then the lesson closing will occur immediately following the lesson body.

<u>Write</u>:

- ✎ a strategy for closing the lesson — Frequently selected strategies for closing the direct instruction lesson are a review of key points of the lesson; a description of where or when students would use their new skills or knowledge; a time for students to show their work; or a reference to the opening. Plans which involve students in the closing are especially effective.

Component 7 - <u>EVALUATION</u>

The *evaluation* component of the direct instruction lesson was planned when the measurable lesson objective was written. Evaluation is designed to determine *individual* student progress in relation to the lesson objective — which means the student does not receive help, from peers or teachers, during the evaluation. Careful monitoring of progress, during supervised and extended practice activities, will help determine when students are ready to be evaluated.

<u>Write</u>:

- ✎ a description of the evaluation — You may want to include a sample in the case of a paper and pencil test and may want to tell when the evaluation will occur if not immediately following the lesson.

Component 8 - <u>EDITING TASKS</u>

This component suggests the following ways to evaluate and complete the first draft of the lesson plan.

- ▸ Examine each component to make sure all are congruent; i.e., all match; rewrite as necessary.
- ▸ Evaluate your use of diversity strategies throughout the lesson; write in any additional strategies needed for the whole group or for individuals.

<u>Write</u>:

- ✎ specific behavior management strategies needed — During transitions, whole group instruction, etc. Consider individual student needs for structure, seating, reinforcement, etc.
- ✎ a list of materials and/or equipment needed for this lesson.

STUDY SUGGESTIONS

1. Look up these terms in the appendix:

   active participation
   check for understanding
   demonstration
   feedback
   prerequisite skills/knowledge
   presentation of information
   supervised practice
   task analysis

2. Read the sample lesson plans at the end of this chapter.

3. Write a direct instruction lesson plan. Some topic ideas are: how to write a check; how to punctuate direct quotations. Refer to Chapter 5 as well as to Chapter 7.

REFERENCES

Arends, R.I. *Classroom Instruction and Management*. New York: McGraw-Hill, 1997.

Borich, G. *Effective Teaching Methods*. 3rd ed. Englewood Cliffs, NJ: Merrill, an imprint of Prentice Hall, Inc., 1996.

Carnine, D., J. Silbert, and E.J. Kameenui. *Direct Instruction Reading*. 2nd ed. New York: Macmillan, 1990.

Engelmann, S., and E. Bruner. *Reading Mastery 1/11 Fast Cycle*. Columbus, Ohio: Macmillan/McGraw-Hill, 1995.

Suggested Readings on Strategy Instruction

Arends, R.I. *Classroom Instruction and Management*. Chapter 8. New York: McGraw-Hill, 1997.

Czarnecki, E., D. Rosko, and E. Fine. "How to Call Up Notetaking Skills." *Teaching Exceptional Children, 30*. pp. 14-19. 1998.

Ellis, E.S., D.D. Deshler, B.K. Lenz, J.B. Schumaker, and F.L. Clark. "An Instructional Model for Teaching Learning Strategies." *Focus on Exceptional Children, 23*. pp. 1-24. 1991.

Gleason, M.M., G. Colvin, and A.L. Archer. "Interventions for Improving Study Skills." In G. Stoner, M.R. Shinn, and H.M. Walker (Eds.), *Interventions for Achievement and Behavior Problems*. pp. 137-160. Silver Spring, MD: The National Association of School Psychologists, 1991.

Mastropieri, M.A., and T.E. Scruggs. "Enhancing School Success with Mnemonic Strategies." *Intervention in School and Clinic, 33.* pp. 201-207. 1998.

Rosenshine, B., and C. Meister. "The Use of Scaffolds for Teaching Higher-Level Cognitive Strategies." *Educational Leadership, 49.* pp. 26-33. 1992.

```
┌─────────────────────────────────────────────────────────────────────┐
│            SAMPLE DIRECT INSTRUCTION LESSON PLAN #1                   │
└─────────────────────────────────────────────────────────────────────┘
```

Topic: ASSIGNMENT CALENDARS

PREPLANNING TASKS

CONTENT ANALYSIS:

   task analysis - <u>Completing a Weekly Assignment Calendar</u>
   1. identify assignment that needs to be written on calendar
   2. locate assignment due date on the calendar
   3. write assignment description on due date
   4. list materials needed

OBJECTIVE: Students will write complete entries on a weekly assignment calendar for five consecutive days, without reminders.

OBJECTIVE RATIONALE: A basic school survival skill is meeting assignment deadlines. Students will increase the likelihood of being successful in school if they come prepared for tests and turn papers and other assignments in on time. (*Note:* This lesson will also provide students with practice using a mnemonic device as a memorization strategy. They were recently taught how to develop these devices.)

MATERIALS AND LOGISTICS: Set up overhead projector; check for transparencies, handouts, assignment cards, and poster; write assignment examples on the board.

LESSON SET-UP

The first period bell signifies the beginning of lesson. **(signal for attention)**

Say: "If you have questions during this lesson, remember to raise your hand and wait to be called on before speaking." **(statement of behavior expectations)**

LESSON OPENING

Say: "Raise your hand if you ever experienced something like this. . .
       — You arrive in class and the teacher passes out a test you have forgotten was going to be given. OR. . .
       — You arrive in class and the other students begin passing in a homework assignment that you forgot was due at the beginning of the class period." (Create interest, establish purpose for knowing strategy.)

Say: "Today you're going to learn how to use a weekly assignment calendar to help you keep track of assignments from all of your classes. Being prepared and meeting deadlines is important to teachers and, therefore, to your success in school." (State the objective and objective purpose.)

LESSON BODY

<u>Reminder</u>!!! Start tape recorder. Distribute points as appropriate. (**diversity strategy**)

"I DO IT" (**teacher show and tell**)
1. Show: Transparency of completed assignment calendar. (**demonstration** of product)
   Say: "All information needed to do and turn in assignments on time is there." Point to the three parts in examples (due date, assignment description, materials needed).

2. Name, define, and show examples of each part of the "completing a weekly assignment calendar" task on transparency. (**presentation of information**)

   A. <u>due date</u> — the day or date the assignment is to be turned in (the weekly dates are written at the top of the calendar).
      <u>examples</u>: Friday; June 21; Wednesday; August 28
      <u>nonexamples</u>: the day it was assigned (e.g., Monday); the date it was assigned (e.g., August 25)
      <u>test examples</u>: assigned on Tuesday; turn in on January 15 (ask for thumbs up/down)

   B. <u>assignment description</u> — brief description of the assignment that includes key points of the assignment.
      <u>examples</u>: division worksheet #46; report on Ben Franklin; lab #14 - Photosynthesis; reading - chapter 6 questions, Part A #1-3, Part B #2-8
      <u>nonexamples</u>: math, report, science, reading
      <u>test examples</u>: math page 42, #1-6; test; spelling words in sentences (ask for thumbs up/down)

   C. <u>materials needed</u> — any specialized equipment or materials that are needed to finish the assignment. Be specific.
      <u>examples</u>: class notes from Monday and Tuesday; CD - Grolier's Encyclopedia; reading book; colored pencils
      <u>nonexamples</u>: notes, art supplies, book
      <u>test examples</u>: paper, brain, math book, spelling list (ask for thumbs up/down)

3. Write in four new assignments on blank calendar transparency while thinking aloud the main steps used in completing an assignment calendar. (Use task analysis as a guide.) Write two from examples on the board. Write two from oral assignments given by student reading from an assignment card, pretending to be the teacher. (**demonstration** of process)

LESSON BODY (continued)

4. Show and tell memory device
    A. Show: MAD poster. Talk through using the MAD mnemonic device to help remember the main   steps. If necessary, review how to use a word strategy as a mnemonic for a memory device.   (**diversity strategy**)

    MAD =   **M**aterials needed
                     Assignment description
                     Date due

    B. Say: "The memory word is MAD."
        Ask: "What is the memory word, everyone?"
        Ask: "What will the memory word help you remember?" Call on nonvolunteers.

    C. **Check for understanding** through active response
        1. Cover the poster and ask for choral responses for each part of the mnemonic. If necessary, go back to A and review/repeat.
        2. Cover the poster and ask each student to write down the complete mnemonic — i.e., MAD and the meaning of each letter — on scratch paper and hold up so the teacher can see it. Monitor and give **feedback**. *(Note*: Students will write the mnemonic at the bottom of the assignment calendars that will be passed out later in the lesson.)

"WE DO IT" (**Supervised practice**)
Write in another assignment on transparency with help from the class. Say: "You may call out your ideas." (**whole group supervised practice**)

Pass out assignment calendars. Students write complete MAD mnemonic on bottom of calendar.

Have students write three new assignments — one oral and two written examples — on their calendars; check each student and give corrective feedback. (**individual supervised practice**)

Note: Remember to check on Ken, Kathy, and Claire first to get them started.
            Say: "If you finish before I get there, compare with your partner." (**diversity strategies**)

LESSON CLOSING

Restate lesson objective: "Today you learned a way to keep track of assignments so that you are not caught unprepared."

Review expectations for rest of the current week and the week to follow. See the extended practice and evaluation, Part 2.

EVALUATION (PART 1)

"YOU DO IT"

Say: "Your 'test' for today is to complete two additional entries on your assignment calendar without help. Select any two homework assignments for today and write them correctly on your assignment calendar."

Students will select from assignments listed within the daily schedule written on the board.

Remind students to put papers in the "In" basket on the filing cabinet.
Remind Randi and Michelle to use the steps for "getting my work done" listed on cards on their desks.
(diversity strategy)

EXTENDED PRACTICE

MORE "WE DO IT"

Each time there is an assignment over the next two days, remind students to write it on their calendars; have partners compare entries; spot check for accuracy. At the end of the day, have students check their calendars against yours on the transparency. Gradually fade reminders over the week. Use Susie, Ted, and Tommy as peer helpers.

EVALUATION (PART 2)

MORE "YOU DO IT"

See the objective. The final evaluation for this lesson will come at the end of next week. During all of next week, students' calendars will be checked every day and performance will be recorded. There will be no reminders.

EDITING TASKS

1. Distribute class points for appropriate "on task" behavior, which is defined on a behavior chart in front of the room. Use the tape recorder that beeps at random intervals to determine when and if points are to be awarded. **(specific management strategies)**
2. Have Danny, Steven, and Jake mark point charts on own desks. Have Susie dictate to Ms. Jenkins (instructional assistant). Have Jerell play the role of teacher in reading oral assignments to increase his interest in the lesson. **(individual accommodations)**

Materials and equipment needed are:
- 26 assignment calendars
- transparency of completed calendar. Include humorous examples (e.g., by Friday, arrange a picnic   with the man on the moon; you will need fried chicken and a rocket ship).
- transparency of a blank calendar
- transparency of names, definitions, etc.
- 10 assignment examples written on board for use in demonstrations and practice. This is more than   needed but use in case students are having trouble.
- poster of MAD mnemonic
- two "oral" assignments written on cards

Note: You will write less detailed plans as you gain experience, when you know the content very well, or when the lesson to teach is fairly short and simple.

When a very detailed plan is written, it may be difficult to use when actually in front of the students. Finding your place can be a problem because, of course, you do not want to read the plan to the students. There are ways you can deal with this. Some teachers find it useful to go back through the plan and highlight only the key points. Others write the key elements in some form — perhaps a list — on a separate piece of paper or on 3" X 5" cards. You may need to experiment until you come up with a method that works well for you. The most important thing is that the lesson goes smoothly.

The following is one example of a plan that could be used when actually presenting the lesson to the students. The main ideas from the detailed plan were put in list form. (See Sample Direct Instruction Lesson Plan #1.)

Topic: ASSIGNMENT CALENDARS

- Before class, write the assignment examples on board.
- Signal.
- Remind: Raise hands during lesson.
- Today, you'll learn - weekly assignment calendar - helps you be prepared.
- Start tape recorder.
- Transp. #1 - completed calendar.
- Transp. #2 - names, definitions, examples, etc. - thumbs up/down.
- Transp. #3 - blank calendar - think out loud (Jerell and cards).
- MAD poster - CFU (check for understanding).
- Transp #3 - blank calendar - write in with class help - call outs okay.
- Hand out calendars - write 3 for practice (check on students; Ms. Jenkins and Susie).
- Today you learned. . .
- Explain extended practice and evaluate, part 2.
- Test - write 2 more.

Topic: MEASURING IN INCHES

Note: You will write less detailed plans as you gain experience, when you know the content very well, or when the lesson to teach is fairly short and simple.

The following is an example of a plan that required less detail when it was originally written because it has simple content and is a short lesson. This plan could double as one to be used in front of the students. The editing tasks component has been placed on the first page with the preplanning tasks to help keep things simple.

PREPLANNING TASKS

CONTENT ANALYSIS
  task analysis:
    1. locate 0 line on a 12" ruler
    2. match the 0 line to the left edge of the line being measured
    3. locate the right end of the line to determine the line length

OBJECTIVE: On a worksheet, students will accurately measure eight lines of varying lengths — in exact inch increments — up to 12 inches.

OBJECTIVE RATIONALE: There are many life applications for measuring with rulers, yardsticks, and tape measures (e.g., constructing game pieces; making book jackets for a favorite book; cutting liner paper for inside school locker; etc.).

EDITING TASKS

Review specific expectations for handling rulers (e.g., for measuring, not for sword fighting). (**specific management strategies**)

Remind Darin to ask Kristen for help, if needed. Highlight line lengths on Kathy's and Don's worksheets, using various colors. (**individual modifications**)

Materials and equipment needed are:
   - see-through 12 inch ruler
   - transparency #1 - line lengths of <u>exactly</u> 4", 7", and 11"
   - transparency #2 - line lengths of <u>exactly</u> 3", 6", and 12"
   - nineteen 12 inch rulers
   - worksheet of 12 line lengths — one for each length 1" through 12" — mixed up
   - transparency #3 - a copy of students' worksheet

LESSON SET-UP

Say: "Simon says look and listen." **(signal for attention)**

Say: "Desks cleared; eyes on teacher or task." **(statement of behavior expectations)**

LESSON OPENING

Create interest - Pose the problem: need to buy paper for book jackets; how much needed depends on book size; how can you find that out?; by measuring them. You'll learn how today.

State objective - "Learn to measure any length up to 12 inches."

Objective purpose - Other examples: liner paper; placemats for a class party. Have students generate their own ideas; call on a few students; then have the rest say their idea to a partner.

LESSON BODY

"I DO IT" (presentation of information/demonstration)

1.   Show: Transparency #1. Explain how to locate 0 line, match it to the line being measured and "read" length. Do several examples while saying the steps out loud. Point to three steps on board. (See the task analysis.)

2.   Show: Transparency #2. *Have one student explain how to measure the first length as I follow the directions on the overhead.

   *Have two students come to overhead and explain/model how to do second and third lengths.

   *Have other students watch for accuracy and prepare for giving feedback. Have them signal (thumbs up/down) whether they agree or disagree. **(checking for understanding)**

"WE DO IT" (supervised practice)

   A.   PASS OUT RULERS. Quickly review handling of rulers — do's and don'ts.

   B.   Show transparency #3. PASS OUT WORKSHEET — which is the same as transparency #3. Answers are to be written in the box next to each line.

3.   Students do first four lines individually. I monitor and provide **feedback**.

LESSON CLOSING

Students come up and write in the correct answers on the transparency. Then, steps are quickly reviewed, one more time.

EVALUATION

"YOU DO IT"

Students complete the last eight examples on the worksheet independently. There is no help from anyone.

EXTENDED PRACTICE

There will be review practice in the next lesson which is on measuring lengths to the one-half inch.

Examples of lengths to the inch and half inch will be mixed.

Future activity will be measuring and making book covers.

Chapter 8

Informal Presentation

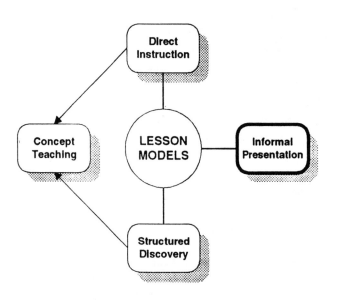

INTRODUCTION

The purpose of the informal presentation model is to deliver information to students in a clear and concise manner. The teacher tells the students what they *are going to be told*; then *tells* them; and finally tells them what they *were told* (Moore, 1994, p. 175). Teachers must know how to effectively present information to students, which is why the informal presentation model is such a valuable one. Careful planning can make these lessons effective with either large groups or small groups of students who are of varying ages and abilities (Ornstein, 1990, p. 296).

An effective informal presentation lesson is designed to lead students to a specific objective. The lesson content is delivered in a clear, interesting manner. The main ideas of the lesson are emphasized through the use of an advance organizer (Ausubel, 1960), graphic organizers,

visual aids, etc. Students are actively involved in the lesson in a variety of ways — such as, asking questions, summarizing concepts, discussing key ideas with a partner.

There are several advantages for using this lesson model. One is that students who have reading and/or reading comprehension problems can benefit significantly, as this type of lesson can serve as a compensatory strategy for them. They are able to gain necessary information without having to rely solely on written material. Another advantage is that this model is very time efficient. Large groups as well as small groups of students can be taught the same information at the same time.

USES OF INFORMAL PRESENTATION

The informal presentation lesson model is most frequently used to teach students *about* something rather than how to *do* something (Arends, 1994, p. 252). This model is appropriately used to present a wide range of content topics and serves a number of purposes. The following examples illustrate the variety of uses for the informal presentation model:

▸ Ms. Henshaw includes content about sexually transmitted diseases (STDs) in a unit she teaches as part of her health class curriculum. She begins the unit with an informal presentation lesson on the types of, and criteria used to classify, STDs. In this case, Ms. Henshaw is using this lesson <u>to present new and integrated information.</u>

- Ms. Wines uses an informal presentation lesson to teach her students about various types of cloud formations. This information is to be used as background information for a series of lessons on causes of weather. Ms. Wines is using an informal presentation lesson to teach background information for future lessons.

- Mrs. Davis follows a student reading assignment about the causes of the Civil War with an informal presentation lesson. The purpose of the lesson is to help clarify previously studied information. She clarifies the information her students gained from the reading assignment.

- Mr. Chin prepares an informal presentation lesson to conclude a series of lessons on the civil rights movement. He uses this lesson model to summarize key points, procedures, and/or facts. In this case, he prepares to summarize a number of key points and generalizations for which his students are held responsible.

- Mrs. Brown uses an informal presentation lesson about volcanos — complete with a working model — as an introductory lesson to a unit on land forms. The purpose of the lesson is to teach specific content AND to help create interest in the upcoming unit.

- Ms. Bishop teaches informal presentation lessons on several aspects of computer technology. The computer content changes far more rapidly than student textbooks are replaced, so the information in her textbooks is often outdated. Ms. Bishop reads extensively to stay current in her field, but the written material she reads is not appropriate for her students. In this case, Ms. Bishop used informal presentation lessons to present information not readily available in other sources — e.g., textbooks.

The informal presentation lesson is often used with other methods and activities during the same class period. These are often in the form of extended practice opportunities. They may also be used to help students further process information during the body of the lesson and to increase interest in or enrich the lesson content. They may precede, but generally follow, the presentation itself. The following are examples:

- Ms. Reed delivers a presentation on genetic engineering which is followed by small group discussions of ethical considerations.

- Students complete various "center" activities where they read, write, draw, and interview peers about their families. Mrs. Bedell then presents basic information about different types of families around the world.

- Mrs. Cline presents information about cell division. Students then go to their lab stations to perform experiments.

- Mr. Springer teaches an informal presentation lesson about parts of a research paper. Students then go to the library to begin collecting resources for their own papers.

- Cooperative groups brainstorm scenarios about emergencies prior to Mrs. Wood's presentation on using 911.

KEY PLANNING CONSIDERATIONS

Informal presentation lessons are not difficult to plan *if* the teacher begins with a thorough understanding of the content to present. When beginning to plan the lesson, special consideration must be given to the following:

Content Knowledge

Preservice teachers often find themselves in the position of being asked to teach lessons on a variety of topics they have never taught before.

When the informal presentation model is used, thorough content knowledge is absolutely essential.

It is necessary to understand how the current content fits into the knowledge structure of the discipline from which it comes. This is because all disciplines have key concepts, information, and generalizations that define them as distinct from other disciplines. These concepts form a knowledge structure — perhaps best conceptualized as one enormous subject matter outline — which provides an organized way to think about and study the information within the discipline; e.g., to categorize it and to show relationships among categories (Arends, 1994, p. 250). When content from a particular discipline is to be taught, it is learned best if students can see how it fits into the "big picture." The *advance organizer* can be used to help explain this "big picture."

The content must be known thoroughly. It would be difficult, if not impossible, to prepare a complete, accurate presentation outline for use in the lesson if the selected subject matter is not fully understood. The success of the presentation delivery would be questionable at best. When an informal presentation lesson is being planned, it is important to do your homework — become an "expert." This will help in choosing interesting and meaningful examples; making relevant comparisons; connecting information to real life applications; asking and answering important questions; and avoiding teaching isolated facts.

Presentation Outline

The *presentation outline* used during the lesson body of the informal presentation lesson is the *subject matter outline* completed during the preplanning tasks component. It must be carefully planned.

Careful preparation of the presentation outline can benefit you and the students. First, it can help ensure that content is selected that directly relates to the objective to be accomplished as well as the knowledge structure of the discipline. (See content

knowledge.) It can also help prevent errors in accuracy and, hopefully, ensure that the information to be presented is clear.

A carefully written presentation outline can be an excellent resource for the students. You may choose to show the outline to the students during the actual presentation or to give them a copy, or partial copy, to use as a note-taking guide. Another option would be to give them the outline to use as a study guide. They can add more information to it from readings, interviews, videos, or other sources.

There is no set rule about the amount of detail to include in the outline. There should be enough detail to ensure a clear presentation; not so much detail that the presentation loses focus because it cannot be followed. You should strive to prepare an outline that is detailed, yet brief. Single words and short phrases serve as cues for information that has been committed to memory. These are preferred to lengthy sentences or narrative (Esler & Sciortino, 1991, p. 98). The outline should serve as a reminder of what will be said and is not to be read.

Advance Organizer

In an informal presentation lesson, the *advance organizer* may be seen as the equivalent of the chapter introduction in a textbook. It may be a picture, a diagram, and/or a verbal explanation (Arends, 1997, p. 247). It contains a key idea or generalization into which the information to come will fit, and it gives students a way to think about that information. An example of a verbal advance organizer is, "There are many types of families, but they all have in common the caring for and support of individual members." Designing the organizer can help evaluate whether or not the presentation is coherent and tied to important key ideas or generalizations.

The advance organizer will be presented during the lesson opening. This will often follow the use of a strategy that helps tie the information to come to prior knowledge. The organizer itself is important information, and it may be necessary to directly teach that information (Joyce, Weil, & Showers, 1992, p. 188). Visual aids and/or graphic organizers may be used to help more clearly explain or demonstrate the content of the advance organizer, if needed.

The following are examples of advance organizers:

- Mrs. Dyson explains to her students that opera themes reflect the composer's interpretation of the social climate of the time.

- Mrs. Donahue opens her presentation on the westward movement by stating, "Human migration follows new economic opportunities and/or political upheavals."

- Mr. Lundquist explains the commonalities among sonatas prior to playing recordings by various composers.

- Ms. Thomas shows a diagram of drugs classified into six types — stimulants, depressants, hallucinogens, inhalants, narcotics, and cannabis products — before providing information about specific drugs.

Presentation Length

The length of the presentation will depend on the students. Two factors to consider are age and attention span. In a primary classroom, the limit for this type of lesson may be five minutes, while, in a high school classroom, the teacher's presentation may last fifteen minutes (Ornstein, 1990, p. 298).

Presentation Delivery

The delivery of this lesson is unique because the teacher is "on stage." A good way to prepare for this type of lesson is to practice the delivery before it is presented to the students. You could either practice in front of a mirror or teach the lesson to the empty classroom after school. Strive for movement around the room, as well as varied voice inflections, facial expressions, and gestures.

Checks for Understanding

A variety of techniques could be used to *check for understanding*. These checks should occur throughout the presentation and just prior to students moving to extended practice or other activities. There are many *active participation* strategies appropriate for this purpose. For example, you could periodically stop during the presentation and ask students to write summary statements or have students use response cards to signal agreement or disagreement. The important thing is to make sure that students do not leave the presentation with misinformation or misunderstandings.

* * * * * * * * * * * * * * * * * * *

81

Figure 8.1 WRITING AN INFORMAL PRESENTATION LESSON

The content of the components below tells what typically would be included in each component in an informal presentation lesson plan. When you write your plan, clearly label each component — e.g., Component 1 - Preplanning Tasks — and component parts — e.g., content analysis, objective.

Component 1 - <u>PREPLANNING TASKS</u>

The *preplanning tasks* section is a cover sheet for the rest of the lesson plan.
<u>Write</u>:
- a *content analysis* — Generally includes a *subject matter outline* (will become the presentation outline), *key terms/vocabulary*, necessary *prerequisite skills/knowledge*.
- an *objective* — In addition to the content objective, a strategy objective may be included (e.g., taking notes from a lecture).
- an *objective rationale* — To help students know why the lesson is valuable.
- Think about the lesson process and diversity strategies to be included.

Component 2 - <u>LESSON SET-UP</u>

<u>Write</u>:
- a *signal for attention* — e.g., turn on overhead projector, ring a bell, raise your hand.
- a *statement of behavior expectations* — e.g., "Please raise your hand before speaking."

Component 3 - <u>LESSON OPENING</u>

A lesson *opening* should be planned carefully, so it will effectively prepare the students for the new learning. An *advance organizer* is an integral part of the lesson opening.
<u>Write</u>:
- a strategy designed to generate interest in the lesson and/or to relate new learning to prior knowledge
- a way to *state the objective*, so students know exactly what they will be expected to know/do
- a statement of the *objective purpose*, so students know why the new learning is valuable and/or useful
- an *advance organizer* and a plan for presenting it. A *graphic organizer* may also be included

---

Component 4 - <u>LESSON BODY</u>

The *lesson body* is the detailed presentation outline — i.e., the subject matter outline prepared as a preplanning task — along with questions, active participation strategies, and checks for understanding.
<u>Write</u>:
- the *presentation outline* — i.e., use the subject matter outline.
- a plan for making the presentation delivery smooth and interesting — e.g., use of voice variations, humor, interesting examples and analogies, summaries.
- techniques that will be used to *check for understanding*. Plan relevant and stimulating questions in advance.

82

Component 4 - LESSON BODY (continued)
✎ diversity strategies for use throughout lesson body. Options:
1. *__graphic organizers__* - (a) provide students with study guides prior to the presentation —include key terms, vocabulary, key ideas; (b) provide students with outlines (complete or partial); (c) use charts, diagrams, or cognitive maps to illustrate important points/concepts; (d) show an outline of the presentation on the overhead; uncover new information as it is introduced.
2. note-taking helps - (a) include a note-taking objective into the lesson — i.e., teach and give feedback on note-taking skills; (b) teach students strategies for note-taking, such as using a new page for each new topic; (c) use cues in the delivery to help students identify key ideas and/or important points (e.g., "Write down this definition in your notes." "The first three ... are."); (d) stop at certain points during the presentation and give students an opportunity to review their notes and ask questions; (e) repeat key points.
3. *visual aids* - video clips, CD segments, slides, posters, charts.
4. other *active participation* strategies - such as reviewing notes with a partner.

Component 5 - EXTENDED PRACTICE

The informal presentation is often used in conjunction with other teaching methods or activities within the same lesson — e.g., presentation followed by a discussion; presentation followed by a writing assignment. All **extended practice** opportunities must relate directly to the lesson objective and the information presented in the lesson body. Individual practice is always the *final* step of this component because students will be evaluated on their individual performance in relation to the lesson objective. You will need to monitor these assignments or activities carefully so you will know when formal evaluation should occur.
Write:
✎ a plan for providing extended practice immediately following the presentation or within a day or two. The following are some extended practice options: assigning related readings; watching a video about the topic presented; gathering additional information by doing library research; conducting experiments in the lab; developing questions using the information presented to be used in a team game; participating in a debate.

Component 6 - LESSON CLOSING

The lesson **closing** generally follows the lesson body if the extended practice activity is a homework assignment. The closing could also occur after extended practice if practice opportunities are to be completed in class immediately following the lesson body. The closing would then follow the in-class practice.
Write:
✎ a strategy for closing the lesson. Frequently selected closing strategies for the presentation lesson are referring back to the opening (e.g., the advance organizer) and reviewing the key points of the lesson. One or more of the following may also be added to the closing: (a) a preview of future learning; (b) a description of where or when students should use the new knowledge; (c) giving students a final opportunity to ask questions; (d) allowing students to compare their notes with a partner.

Component 7 - <u>EVALUATION</u>

The lesson *evaluation* could occur immediately after the presentation with a paper and pencil test. It more commonly occurs after the use of other methods (e.g., discussion) and/or extended practice opportunities are provided. The careful monitoring of activities that occur after the actual informal presentation will tell you when students are ready for the lesson evaluation. The evaluation specified in the lesson objective is used to "test" individual student attainment of the specific objective.

<u>Write</u>:

✎ a description of the evaluation.

Component 8 - <u>EDITING TASKS</u>

This component provides a way to evaluate and complete the first draft of the lesson plan.

▸ Examine each component to make sure all are congruent — i.e., all match — rewrite as necessary.

▸ Evaluate the use of diversity strategies throughout the lesson; write in any additional strategies needed for the whole group or for individuals.

<u>Write</u>:

✎ specific management strategies needed — e.g., during the presentation (i.e., whole group instruction), during transitions from the presentation portion of the lesson to other methods or activities (e.g., lab work), etc. You may need to consider the seating arrangement, making sure that students who have the most difficult time remaining involved in lessons are closest to you.

✎ a list of materials/equipment needed for this lesson — e.g., posters, audio-visual equipment, CD player and CDs, real objects.

Practice, practice, practice the delivery before presenting to the students!

STUDY SUGGESTIONS

1. Look up these terms in the appendix:

   active participation
   advance organizer
   check for understanding
   graphic organizer
   key terms/vocabulary
   presentation outline
   subject matter outline
   visual aids

2. Read the sample lesson plans at the end of this chapter.

3. Write an informal presentation lesson plan. Some topic ideas are: volcanoes, different types of families, the three branches of government. Refer to Chapter 5 as well as to Chapter 8.

REFERENCES

Ausubel, D.P. "The Use of Advance Organizers in the Learning and Retention of Meaningful Verbal Material." *Journal of Educational Psychology, 51.* pp. 267-272. 1960.

REFERENCES AND SUGGESTED READINGS

Arends, R.I. *Learning to Teach.* 3rd ed. Chapter 8. New York: McGraw-Hill, 1994.

Arends, R.I. *Classroom Instruction and Management.* New York: McGraw-Hill, 1997.

Callahan, J.F., L.H. Clark, and R.D. Kellough. *Teaching in the Middle and Secondary Schools.* 5th ed. Part 111, Module 9. New Jersey: Merrill, 1995.

Esler, W.K. and P. Sciortino. *Methods for Teaching: An Overview of Current Practices.* 2nd ed. Chapter 6. Raleigh, NC: Contemporary Publishing Company, 1991.

Joyce, B., M. Weil, and B. Showers. *Models of Teaching.* 4th ed. Chapter 9. Boston: Allyn and Bacon, 1992.

Lorber, M.A. and W.D. Pierce. *Objectives, Methods and Evaluation for Secondary Teaching.* 3rd ed. Chapter 4. Englewood Cliffs: Prentice Hall, 1990.

Moore, K.D. *Secondary Instructional Methods.* Chapter 7. Madison: Brown & Benchmark, 1994.

Ornstein, A.C. *Strategies for Effective Teaching.* Chapter 6. New York: Harper & Row, 1990.

SAMPLE PRESENTATION LESSON PLAN #1

Topic: **COMPREHENSIVE EFFECTS OF ADDICTION**

PREPLANNING TASKS

CONTENT ANALYSIS:

subject matter outline - (See presentation outline below.)

key terms/vocabulary -

physical dependence - when a person's body becomes used to the presence of a drug and cannot function without it

emotional dependence - believing that one cannot face life without drugs/alcohol

prerequisite skills/knowledge - know the definition of abuse, dependence, and addiction, and how to take notes from a lecture

OBJECTIVE: From memory, students will write examples of the comprehensive effects of drug and alcohol abuse. Two examples from each of five major categories of effects — e.g., dependence, economic, family, social, academic — must be included.

OBJECTIVE RATIONALE: Students must be aware of the detrimental effects of drug and alcohol abuse (a) to help them make informed choices about their personal use/nonuse and (b) so they may recognize symptoms in others as a first step in giving or getting help for the individual in need.

LESSON SET-UP

Turn on overhead projector. The light signals students to turn and face me. **(signal for attention)**

Say: "It's time to begin our health lesson. It is important that you listen carefully and take notes as I present information. Remember that if you have questions, please raise your hand and wait to be called on before talking. I will stop several times during my presentation so that you have a chance to check your notes and ask additional questions." **(statement of behavior expectations)**

LESSON OPENING

Note: I've written out detailed narrative for the opening to help me thoroughly think through how I will introduce this important topic.

Say: We've been studying drug and alcohol abuse for the past several days. You will remember that continued abuse can lead to addiction and that, when addiction occurs, the user's top priority in life becomes the drug." **(review)**

Say: "Today and tomorrow I am going to tell you about some specific problems that result from drug and alcohol addiction. It is important for you to know about the specific effects that can result from the abuse of drugs and alcohol, so that you can make an informed personal choice regarding drug and alcohol use. Secondly, it is important to know these effects so that you are able to recognize symptoms of drug and alcohol addiction in those around you. Recognizing that a problem exists is the first step in solving it." **(state the objective and objective purpose)**

LESSON OPENING (continued)

Show transparency #1 — a diagram of problem categories. **(advance organizer)**

Say: "Before I present you with specific examples of problems that can be caused by drug and alcohol abuse, you need to know the following:

    1. Drug and alcohol abuse causes comprehensive problems and affects all facets of a person's life.

    2. Specific problems caused by drug and alcohol abuse can be sorted into the following categories: dependence (physical and emotional), economic, family, social, academic."

Think-Pair-Share — everything you already know about the problems that drugs and alcohol can cause. **(diversity strategy)**

Show transparency #2 — an outline with main category headings.

Say: "At the end of my presentation, you will be able to write specific examples of problems caused by drug and alcohol abuse within each of these general categories. As I present information, you will fill in the details of this outline." **(diversity strategy)**

Say: "Remember the skits on drug and alcohol abuse we're going to write and act out next week. This lesson will give you lots of ideas."

LESSON BODY (taught on two consecutive days)

(presentation delivery) - Move around room; make eye contact with ALL students. Remember to use verbal cues to help students identify key ideas and/or important points; e.g., "The first problem category......" Stop after each category for brief summary. I have also included interesting case studies to illustrate key points of my presentation. **(diversity strategies)**

(individual modifications) - (1) Provide Jan with an outline that includes major headings and subheadings. (2) Ask John to review notes with Ada.

Refer to transparency #2 on the overhead. Cover all but the first heading.

1. <u>dependence</u>
    A. physical problems
        1. addiction
        2. tolerance increases
    B. emotional problems
        *cannot face life without the drug
    C. the case of Charlotte M.

2. economic problems
    A. cost of addiction can be hundreds of dollars each day
    B. problems on the job (U.S. economy loses $71,200,000 a day due to drug abuse)
        1. decline in productivity
            *inconsistent performance
        2. increase of absence due to illness (drug related)
        3. decline in reliability
        4. mistakes on the job
            a. poor decision making
            b. higher rate of accidents
        5. may steal money for drugs
    C. loss of job (Show video clip #1 - "The Firing.")
    D. the case of Monty R.

Say: "Take the next three minutes to compare your notes with someone next to you. Fill in whatever information is missing." **(diversity strategy)** Ask for questions. Ask several students at random: "What is an example of an economic problem caused by drug and alcohol abuse? caused by a dependence problem?"

Present more information.

3. family problems
    A. arguments about drinking; tries to convince the person to stop drinking
        *family feels angry and hurt (Show video clip #2 - "I Hate You!")
    B. decline in reliability, dependability
    C. loss of interest in family activities
    D. mood swings
    E. abuse of other family members
        1. relationship between alcoholism and domestic violence (child abuse and spouse or partner abuse)
        2. emotional abuse
        3. physical abuse
    F. theft from family members
        *mistrust and anger
    G. the case of Jimmy D.

Stop for questions and comments

4. social problems
    A. classmates and/or friends resent individual's lack of effort, failure to cooperate
    B. personality changes
    C. friendships end (Show video clip #3 - "My Dog Still Loves Me.")
    D. the case of Donny J.

LESSON BODY (continued)

5. academic problems
   - A. attendance drops
   - B. concentration difficult
   - C. poor study habits; e.g., unfinished homework
   - D. grades decline
   - E. drop out
   - F. the case of Shirley M.

Say: "Now compare the rest of your notes with someone next to you. Fill in whatever information is missing." Ask for any final questions.

LESSON CLOSING

Show transparency of advance organizer again and review the key points — i.e., categories of problems. Do this at the end of each day. **(review)**

Restate why this information is important for students to know. **(restate objective purpose)**

EXTENDED PRACTICE (following second day)

Say: "Your homework assignment for tonight is to read pages 35-45 in your health book. These pages give additional examples and information pertaining to the categories of problems caused by drug and alcohol abuse. Be prepared to discuss the information you read during class tomorrow."

Say: "Also make notes in your journal about skit ideas/scenes."

EVALUATION

1. At the beginning of class tomorrow, I'll have students write down (from memory) at least two specific examples from at least five categories.
2. There will be a test on the drug and alcohol abuse unit. The short answer question pertaining to the information today will be:
   "Drug and alcohol addiction causes comprehensive problems for the user. List at least two specific examples for at least five general categories of problems caused by drug and alcohol abuse."

EDITING TASKS

"Check in" with Cody and Brittany more frequently. Proximity helps them stay focused. **(specific management strategy)**

graphic organizers **(materials/equipment)**
   - a. transparency of advance organizer (#1) - shows categories and comprehensive and interrelated effects of drug abuse
   - b. transparency of presentation outline - major headings only (#2)
   - c. outline for Jan - headings and subheadings

SAMPLE PRESENTATION LESSON PLAN #2

Topic: BASIC CLOUD TYPES

PREPLANNING TASKS

CONTENT ANALYSIS:
    subject matter outline - (See presentation outline.)
    key terms/vocabulary - cumulus, stratus, cirrus - defined in presentation outline

OBJECTIVE: On a worksheet, students will match cloud names (stratus, cirrus, cumulus) with written descriptions of appearance and location in the sky.

OBJECTIVE RATIONALE: Students need to know the three basic types of clouds (stratus, cirrus, cumulus) because all other clouds are made from these three types. This lesson provides background information necessary for the main ideas of lessons to come: (1) All clouds are made of combinations of the three basic types, and (2) Cloud appearance and location in the sky are two factors that can be used to predict weather patterns.

LESSON SET-UP

Begin mime movements; students imitate. **(signal for attention)**

*Move students from tables to rug. Excuse as ready. Wait on rug and immediately begin acknowledging students who are displaying "appropriate" rug behavior.

Remind of personal space on rug; eyes on the speaker or activity; raise hand for comments/questions. **(statement of behavior expectations)**

LESSON OPENING

Show: Video clip of various cloud formations filmed with time lapse photography, very fast paced and dramatic in appearance. **(generate interest)**

Explain the **(advance organizer)**.
Say: "All clouds are variations of three basic types"
Say: "Believe it or not...all of the clouds you have just seen are made from three basic kinds of clouds." (Show poster of clouds and relative position.)

Say: "Today you will learn the names of the three basic clouds — how they look and where they are located in the sky." **(statement of objective)**

Explain **objective purpose**. This information will help in future lessons when you learn about the clouds you saw on the video tape and others. You'll also learn how the appearance of clouds and their location in the sky influences the weather.

LESSON BODY

Note: My personal goals for the presentation delivery are the following: (1) to scan so I'm aware of what all students are doing, and (2) to make eye contact with ALL students.

Tell students I will stop after telling about each cloud type so they may review the information with a partner. **(diversity strategy)**
    *Refer students to and quickly review the partner work T-chart (looks like, sounds like) in front of the room. Special reminder of encouraging; give examples.

(presentation outline)
1. <u>Three Main Types of Clouds</u> - Show poster of three basic cloud types — cloud heights from sea level and cloud appearance very clear.
    A. **cirrus** - means "to curl," often called "mares' tails," feather.
        Show poster and photographs - variations of cirrus clouds.
        1. appearance — wispy, fibrous, thin, curved, curled
        2. location in sky — high in the sky; 7+ miles high

STOP: Have students tell partners cloud name, location, and appearance.
Say: "See if you can help each other think of a way to remember the important information about the cloud; e.g., cirrus sounds like "circus;" could make you think of mares' tails, feathers."
*Remind students about encouragement; reference T-chart that addresses partner work. **(monitor partners)**
Have individual students show true/false cards following statements I make about cirrus clouds. **(check for understanding)**

Say: "<u>Freeze</u>." (I'll use the stronger signal here because during partner work the noise level is a bit louder than usual.) Continue with presentation.

    B. **cumulus** - means "to gather together," heap.
        Refer to poster. Show photographs; variations of cumulus clouds.
        1. appearance — fluffy, look like cotton, textured
        2. location in sky — lower part of the sky, approximately 3 miles

STOP: Do partner work. Possible memory word - accumulate.
Show true/false cards. **(check for understanding)**
Say: "<u>Freeze</u>." Continue with presentation.

    C. **stratus** - means "layer."
        Refer to poster. Show photographs; variations of stratus clouds.
        1. appearance — flat, thick, gray clouds appear to cover the sky
        2. location in sky — very low in the sky, up to 1 mile high, less (fog)

STOP: Do partner work. Possible memory word - straight.
Show true/false cards. **(check for understanding)**
Say: "<u>Freeze</u>." Move to closing.

LESSON CLOSING

1. Tell students about tomorrow's science lesson where they will begin looking up information about other types of clouds which are made up of combinations of these three. They'll be able to reference books and the World Wide Web. **(preview future lessons)**
2. Show poster again. Verbally review for students the appearance and location of the three cloud types. **(review)**
3. Students show true/false cards in response to statements about all three cloud types.

EXTENDED PRACTICE

I will reinforce information about the three basic cloud types in several ways prior to evaluation.

1. The after lunch story is used to extend information from various curriculum areas. Today I'll read "The Clouds Above Us" by Tom Springer to reinforce cloud types.
2. Today in science I will show the video tape called "Help! It's Raining and a Labrador Retriever Just Fell on My Head!"

EVALUATION

Student progress will be evaluated as part of the daily opening activities tomorrow morning. Students will be given a worksheet where they will need to match the cloud name with a written description of its appearance and location in the sky.

EDITING TASKS

*When moving students to the rug, be sure that John and Sherry are close to me. Have Larry and Tammy work as partners. **(specific management strategies)**

(materials/equipment)
advance organizer
a. poster of three basic cloud types
b. video clip and VCR
visual aids
a. large poster that shows cloud heights from sea level, designed so that cloud appearance (e.g., cumulus clouds are puffy) and sky position of each are easy to see (e.g., stratus cloud is in a 'low' position)
b. photographs of variations of three basic cloud types
c. 24 worksheets
other
true/false cards

Chapter 9

Structured Discovery

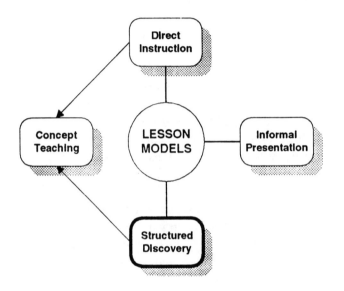

INTRODUCTION

The structured discovery model is one in which students "discover" information rather than having it told to them. The discovery from the lesson is a planned one, however; i.e., students discover a correct answer. What they discover is the lesson objective which is predetermined by the teacher. Students are led to the specific objective in a convergent rather than divergent manner. Structured discovery utilizes an inductive rather than deductive approach to learning. This model will help round out the repertoire of beginning skills needed to plan lessons.

Structured discovery lessons have a number of similarities to direct instruction lessons. The purpose of both lesson models is for students to reach a specific academic objective. The major difference between them is the *route* that students take to reach the objective. The lesson body is where the most significant differences between the two models are found. In the structured discovery lesson, the teacher prepares the students for discovery by presenting examples and nonexamples for them to explore. In a direct instruction lesson, the teacher is telling and showing the information that the students need to know in order to reach the objective. The rest of the lesson body is quite similar in both types of lessons. The teacher follows the students discovery by summarizing, reviewing, and/or providing additional practice with the new learning (supervised practice). The same methods also follow the show and tell portion of the body in a direct instruction lesson.

Structured discovery is often confused with the inquiry method or model. They might look the same to a novice teacher, so we have provided information to help distinguish between them. Students "discover" in both models, but the purpose and outcome of the discovery vary significantly. The major goal of structured discovery is for students to learn academic content, while the major goal of inquiry is for students to experience and practice the actual *process* of making a discovery (Arends, 1994, p. 369). For example, students may do air pressure experiments in order for them to discover facts about air pressure. On the other hand, the goal may be for students to practice making accurate scientific observations. In this case, magnetism, or some topic other than air pressure, might have been selected because the topic is solely a vehicle for having students practice observing. In the first example, an objective would be written that focused on knowledge of air pressure. In the second case, the objective would be written for the skill of making observations and would be a long term objective. Therefore, inquiry fits the definition of an activity rather than a lesson.

Understanding the intent of the structured discovery model lays the foundation for using it successfully. The previous paragraphs have described what structured discovery *is* and how it compares to other models. The following tells what structured discover is *not*. It is NOT a lesson without purpose or focus. It does NOT create a setting where students randomly experiment with materials or information. It also is NOT a time when students are encouraged to come up with any "creative" idea or conclusion that comes to mind. A teacher would NOT be successful if students had a great deal of fun "discovering" but did not discover the information needed for the next day's science lesson. Structured discovery is a model to be selected when *content* knowledge is to be taught. The lesson process is an added benefit — a secondary objective — not the major one.

USES OF STRUCTURED DISCOVERY

The primary objective in a structured discovery lesson is always an academic one. The teacher may be teaching facts, concepts, academic rules, scientific laws, etc. Some examples of specific topics are defining a noun; rules for punctuation; what magnets will pick up; emergencies when you should call 911; and typical locations of cities.

There are several reasons why a structured discovery lesson may be selected to teach particular academic content. One reason is increased student motivation. The challenge of "making the discovery" can create an exciting situation for the students and, therefore, will hold their attention more easily. When preparing to

teach a topic that students may consider to be uninteresting — e.g., a specific grammar rule —using a structured discover lesson should be considered. It might provide just the right motivation.

A second reason why a structured discovery lesson may be selected is because it promotes higher level thinking skills. Most educators agree that all students in school need opportunities to develop their ability to reason and solve problems. Structured discovery lessons are one way to provide this practice. Older students and/or those with intellectual gifts may need even more of these opportunities and will likely be especially excited and challenged by structured discovery lessons. *Note*: In addition to the primary academic objective, you may wish to include a long term objective that addresses "thinking" — e.g., problem solving, analysis, asking relevant questions, drawing conclusions — in the lesson plan.

A third reason to use a structured discovery lesson is that it may enhance retention. Students may be more apt to recall what they have learned when they have been given the opportunity to figure out something for themselves.

Structured discovery lessons are a valuable teaching tool, but they are not always appropriate. This type of lesson should obviously never be used when the safety of students is an issue. It would not make sense, for instance, to have students discover how to use a Bunsen-burner safely or how to effectively break a fall from a balance beam. Additionally, this type of lesson would not be used when damage to materials or equipment may result. For example, it would be inappropriate for students to discover how to turn off a computer.

A structured discovery lesson should not be used when student failure to discover is likely. It would not make much sense, for example, to have students discover how to solve long division problems. It is fairly predictable they would flounder in failure as they repeatedly practiced the wrong way to compute long division problems. It may make sense, however, to have them discover math *concepts* such as "division."

A structured discovery lesson would, also, not be a good choice when the time involved in making the discovery outweighs the benefit of the discovery itself. It may be possible, for instance, for students to eventually discover the concept of democracy. However, the time it would take to make such a discovery would most probably decrease the value of making the discovery. Sometimes the time factor makes the use of this model prohibitive.

A thorough content analysis can help determine when a structured discovery lesson would be a good choice. Using some good common sense will help here as well.

KEY PLANNING CONSIDERATIONS

Structured discovery lessons require *very* careful planning in order to help ensure that students will learn information accurately. These lessons have a high probability of resulting in student confusion. Consideration of the following areas is especially important.

Assessing Prerequisite Skills and Knowledge

Lesson readiness can be determined in two steps. First, it is necessary to analyze what the students need to know — i.e., *prerequisite skills/ knowledge* — in order to be successful in the current lesson. Secondly, there must be an assessment as to whether or not they know it. The following is an example: You plan a structured discovery lesson on adjectives. You know that students must be able to identify nouns in order to understand adjectives. Therefore, you test your students on noun identification.

Gathering assessment information can be either fairly easy — e.g., correcting papers from

yesterday's assignment — or more complicated — e.g., writing and administering a formal pretest. However, assessment of individual students must be performed regardless of the level of difficulty.

Writing the Objective

The short term academic objective written for the structured discovery lesson is no different from an objective written for lessons using other models. The important thing to remember about structured discovery objectives is how they should *not* be written. They should not, for example, say something like, "Students will *discover...*" Objectives for all lessons must state what the students will know or do at the end of the lesson. The means to the end is not stated in the objective. (See Chapter 3.)

Selecting Examples and Nonexamples

Examples and nonexamples for these lessons must be carefully selected because of the potential for confusion during the discovery phase. It is best to start with the clearest, purest examples and nonexamples. Successive examples can be more abstract, more difficult to discriminate. These examples and nonexamples can be in the form of individual problems, words or scenarios, pictures, demonstrations, etc.

Sometimes it is not necessary to include nonexamples. For example, in the adjective lesson at the end of this chapter, nonexamples are not needed because students are not being taught to distinguish between an adjective and other parts of speech. Instead they are discovering the relationship between adjectives and nouns, as well as various categories of adjectives. A careful content analysis will help determine whether or not nonexamples are needed.

Planning Questions and Prompts

It is a good idea to plan in advance how to guide the discovery. What will be done, for example, if students seem completely baffled by the initial explanation and examples? Writing down specific questions, statements, or clues will be beneficial, as they will serve to prompt students' thinking. Visual cues may also be planned.

Supervised Practice

One of the tricky parts of a structured discovery lesson is determining whether or not all of the students have really "discovered." The teacher must take an active role in helping students draw correct conclusions before the end of the lesson. This is followed by having students practice the new learning under the teacher's supervision. It is very important to remember that the part of the lesson where the students "discover" is NOT *supervised practice*. For example, after the students have discovered facts about air pressure, you would want to provide new problems or demonstrations which would allow them to apply the facts they have learned. As students practice, you must monitor to be sure they are using the "discovered" information accurately.

* * * * * * * * * * * * * * * * * * *

Figure 9.1 WRITING A STRUCTURED DISCOVERY LESSON

The content of the components below tells what typically would be included in each component in a structured discovery lesson plan. When you write your plan, clearly label each component — e.g., Component 1 - Preplanning Tasks — and the component parts — e.g., task analysis, objective.

Component 1 - <u>PREPLANNING TASKS</u>

The preplanning tasks section is a cover sheet for the rest of the lesson plan.

<u>Write</u>:

✎ a *content analysis*. This may be a *subject matter outline*, *task analysis* or *concept analysis*, *key terms/vocabulary*, and/or necessary *prerequisite skills/ knowledge*.

✎ an *objective*. Remember that the objective represents the learning outcome, not the learning activities or process. For example, you would not write, "Students will discover..." Possible objectives for a structured discovery lesson could be for students to describe, state a generalization, identify, define, write, give an example.

✎ an *objective rationale* to help you clarify the value of the objective.

▸ Think about the lesson process and diversity strategies to be included.

Component 2 - <u>LESSON SET-UP</u>

The *lesson set-up* is the first component of the lesson plan that is actually presented to students.

<u>Write</u>:

✎ a *signal for attention* — e.g., hand signal; say, "Listen, please."

✎ a *statement of behavior expectations* — e.g., eyes on me, following directions.

Component 3 - <u>LESSON OPENING</u>

The lesson *opening* should effectively prepare the students for the new learning.

Write:
- a strategy designed to generate interest in the lesson and/or to relate new learning to prior knowledge.
- a way to *state the objective* so students know what they will learn. Be careful not to give away the discovery, however.
- a statement of *objective purpose*, so students know why the new learning is valuable and useful.

Component 4 - <u>LESSON BODY</u>

The *lesson body* is a detailed, step-by-step description of the actual teaching to the objective that will be done; i.e., what the teacher and the students will be doing. Always included are *active participation* strategies and monitoring of student progress.

Write:
- the lesson body. In the structured discovery model, you will first present examples and nonexamples and then lead students to discover the definition, rule, etc. you are teaching. *Note:* Be sure to repeat and review — *check for understanding* — the essential learning to ensure that all students "discovered" the correct information. Include *supervised practice* with *feedback* as well.
- diversity strategies throughout the lesson body. Diversity strategies to consider using in structured discovery lessons are to:
  1. provide more structure in the initial presentation of examples; e.g., in the use of cues, concrete objects, leading questions.
  2. give clear directions for how students should share tasks in partner or group work.
  3. repeat/review the correct information to make sure all students "discovered."
  4. elicit many active participation responses.
  5. increase the amount and types of extended practice. (See Component 5.)

Component 5 - <u>EXTENDED PRACTICE</u>

Extended practice opportunities help students develop high enough levels of accuracy and fluency to ensure they can generalize the skill or knowledge. Some students may need a great deal of extended practice while others may need enrichment activities.

Write:
- a plan for providing extended practice immediately following the lesson or soon thereafter.
- a list of lessons or activities that will build on this objective. Any additional opportunities students will have to generalize and extend the information should be included as appropriate. You may have planned a structured discovery lesson to teach information that students will need in a lesson to follow; e.g., today's structured discovery lesson, designed to teach the definition of noun, provides the background information necessary for tomorrow's direct instruction lesson on common and proper nouns.

Component 6 - LESSON CLOSING

The lesson *closing* may follow the body of the lesson or it may follow extended practice.

Write:

✎ a strategy for closing the lesson. You may wish to include a variety of activities into your lesson closing. Options for those activities include: (a) a review of key points of the lesson; (b) opportunities for students to draw conclusions; (c) a description of where or when students should use their new skills or knowledge; (d) a reference to the lesson opening.

Component 7 - EVALUATION

The lesson *evaluation* was planned when the objective was written, so the evaluation must match exactly what is stated in the objective. Remember that evaluation is not necessarily a paper and pencil test. Also, remember that its purpose is to determine how *individual* students are progressing toward the lesson objective, which means the student does not receive help — from peers or teacher — during the evaluation.

The *evaluation* component of the structured discovery lesson was planned when the measurable lesson objective was written. Do not forget to test with new examples. Careful monitoring during supervised and extended practice activities will help decide when evaluation should occur.

Write:

✎ a plan for evaluating whether the learning has occurred.

Component 8 - EDITING TASKS

This component provides a way to evaluate and complete the first draft of the lesson plan.

▸ Examine each component to make sure all are congruent; i.e., that all match. Rewrite as necessary.

▸ Evaluate the use of diversity strategies throughout the lesson. Write in any additional strategies needed for the whole group or for individuals.

Write:

✎ specific management strategies needed. Students often work together in partners or in small groups during the "discovery" portion of the structured discovery lesson. Remember that students may need to be taught and/or reminded of specific behaviors necessary for working successfully in that way. When lessons involve manipulating/sharing materials or equipment, behavioral expectations need to be addressed as well. You may also need to consider students' tolerance for working through feelings of frustration and confusion as the probability of this happening is greater in this type of lesson. Also, consider students' needs regarding seating, reinforcement, etc.

✎ a list of materials/equipment needed for this lesson.

STUDY SUGGESTIONS

1. Review these terms in the appendix:

   active participation
   check for understanding
   closing
   content analysis
   evaluation
   extended practice
   feedback
   opening
   supervised practice

2. Read the sample lesson plans at the end of this chapter.

3. Write a structured discovery lesson plan. Topic ideas could include the following: objects that sink or float; the rules for Haiku poetry. Refer to Chapter 5 as well as to Chapter 9.

SUGGESTED READINGS

Arends, R.I., *Learning to Teach*. 3rd ed. New York: McGraw-Hill. Chapter 12, 1994.

Esler, W.K. and P. Sciortino. *Methods for Teaching: An Overview of Current Practices*. 2nd ed. Raleigh, NC: Contemporary Publishing Company. Chapter 7, 1991.

Joyce, B., M. Weil, and B. Showers. *Models of Teaching*. 4th ed. Boston: Allyn and Bacon. Chapters 6 and 10, 1992.

SAMPLE STRUCTURED DISCOVERY LESSON PLAN #1

Topic: SPELLING PATTERN - FORMING PLURALS OF NOUNS ENDING IN
CONSONANT + Y

PREPLANNING TASKS

CONTENT ANALYSIS:

task analysis - Look at singular form of word; is it a noun? Does it end in y preceded by a consonant? If so, rewrite the word but drop the y. Now add "ies" to form the plural.

prerequisite skills/knowledge - recognition of nouns; recognition of consonants (versus vowels); concept of singular and plural nouns

Note to myself: <u>Need to include examples</u> — where y has different pronunciations (spy, baby); where words have different numbers of syllables (spy, baby, butterfly); where there is a single or double consonant preceding the y (baby, berry) — to make sure students can figure out the exact rule. Only include nouns at this point.

OBJECTIVE: Students will correctly write 10/10 plural forms when given written list of singular nouns, including 6 which end in y preceded by a consonant; e.g., berry - berries. The other words will require simple addition of "s;" e.g., boy - boys.

OBJECTIVE RATIONALE: Students have prerequisite knowledge. Students are using many words which follow this pattern in unit on pets — e.g., pony, bunny, puppy — and do not know how to spell plural forms correctly. This lesson will also reinforce recognition of nouns. Using the structured discovery model gives students more practice on word/pattern analysis.

LESSON SET-UP

Signal: "Give me 5." "Take out your big scratch pad and black marker."
Expectations: "Raise hands before speaking, unless I say, 'Everyone...'"

LESSON OPENING

Say: Today you are going to learn a rule which will help you figure out how to spell certain words by yourself. This rule will help you spell some of the words you are using in our pet unit, like 'puppies' and 'ponies.'

Show: Pictures of animals.

Review: Definitions of noun, singular/plural, consonant/vowel. Review plural forms from previous lessons (farms, toys).

LESSON BODY

Show: Transparency with two columns:

(1)	(2)
bunny - bunnies	boy - boys
city - cities	donkey - donkeys
butterfly - butterflies	day - days

Note: I read the words out loud. Remember to do this throughout the lesson for those who have reading difficulties.

Say: "Look at all of the words in both columns. Think about how *all* of the words are alike. Raise your hand if you know one way they are alike." Call on volunteers; use wait time! If necessary, prompt, "In each pair, the first word is singular and the second is... What part of speech are these words?"

Say: "Now look at all of the singular words." I underline them. "Think about how they are alike." Wait. "Talk to your partner about your idea." Wait; signal for attention. Then call on nonvolunteers. If necessary, prompt, "They all end in the letter...; everyone?"

Say: "Now look at the word pairs in the first column and compare them to the word pairs in the second column. Notice that each column has a different spelling rule for making the plural word. See if you can figure out the rule." Wait. "Now turn to the people in your table group and talk it over." Wait; walk around and listen to the groups. Then call on someone if most figured out the rule OR...
If necessary -

Show: The transparency with these cues:
*Circle the letter preceding the y and elicit that they are consonants in column 1 and vowels in column 2. Ask for a choral response.
*In column 1, cross out the y's in the singular words and underline the "ies" in the plural words. In column 2, underline the y in singular words, underline the ys in the plural words, and elicit the rule. Call on nonvolunteers.

Say: "Notice that the number of syllables doesn't matter, the pronunciation of the y doesn't matter, and single or double consonants before the y doesn't matter." Point to and say examples from the transparency.

Show: The rule written on a poster — To form the plural of nouns ending in y preceded by a consonant, drop the y and add "ies." Ask the class to read it out loud as a group. Call on individuals to paraphrase. Show the steps written on the poster. (See task analysis.) Read out loud as a group.

Say: "Watch me as I use the rule to figure out a new word." Write strawberry on the transparency. I talk through the steps out loud. Repeat for nonexample — Saturday.

LESSON BODY (continued)

supervised practice:

Say: "Let's do one together." Write baby on the transparency. "Tell me what to do, everyone..." Prompt by pointing to steps on the poster. Write the plural on transparency. Repeat with bay.

Say: "Now try two by yourselves." Write donkey and pony on transparency. "Say the steps out loud as you write the plural forms in big letters on your scratch paper. Then hold your paper up so I can see." Monitor.

Say: "Let's practice once more." Remove posters and write penny and tinkertoy on transparency. "This time say the steps in your head. Hold your paper up when you're ready." Monitor.

LESSON CLOSING

Say: "Many times when you are writing about people, animals, places, and things, you want to write about more than one. For example, in your science journals, you might want to write, 'One guppy is hiding in the castle. The other guppies are at the top of the tank eating.' You'll see the word guppy on the sign above the tank." Point to it. "Now you know how to figure out how to write guppies. Tell me, everyone..." Write guppies on the board.

EVALUATION

Hand out test. (See objective.) Words are: cherry, cat, kitty, spy, hobby, Friday, boy, puppy, key, family.

diversity strategy:

Say: "Work by yourselves, please. When you are finished, remember to proofread; put your paper in the spelling box; and then read quietly." *Note:* Reading partners will read the words out loud to those with reading difficulties during the test — so they can recognize the nouns — but not help with writing plurals.

EXTENDED PRACTICE

▸   Remind students of this spelling rule before they write their pet observations in their science journals.

▸   Include examples of words which follow this rule in the spelling list so students learn how to spell the whole word, not just the ending.

EDITING TASKS

specific management strategies:
Remind table groups that they are working on "hearing everyone's ideas" this week. Also, remember to praise Ben and Wally for volunteering answers.

materials/equipment:
- transparencies with examples, cues
- overhead projector
- posters of rule of steps
- pictures of animals

Topic: IDENTIFYING ADJECTIVES

PREPLANNING TASKS

CONTENT ANALYSIS:

concept analysis: *Note*: Only some portions of a concept analysis apply because students are not being taught how to distinguish adjectives from other words.

    <u>name</u> - adjective

    <u>definition</u> - a word that describes a quality or attribute of a noun. It may tell how many — e.g., ten, one — describe physical traits — e.g., color, texture, shape, size, — personality traits, emotions, age, etc.

    <u>critical attributes</u> - tells about the noun

    <u>noncritical attributes</u> - position in relation to the noun in a phrase or sentence; positive or negative trait; type of noun — singular or plural, proper or common.

    <u>examples</u> - friendly, rough, teal, twenty-four, many, ten, blue, round, big, tiny, funny, quiet, shy, happy, serious

    <u>nonexamples</u> - NA

    <u>related concepts</u> - NA

prerequisite knowledge: recognition of nouns in sentences

OBJECTIVES:

specific lesson objective:

    (1) Given 10 phrases and sentences that contain at least one adjective in various positions in relation to the noun, students will identify by circling all adjectives.

goal:

    (2) Students will learn to identify critical attributes of a concept.

OBJECTIVE RATIONALE: The main purposes of this lesson are for students to discover:

    (a) the relationship between an adjective and a noun

    (b) categories of adjectives

    (c) the adjective's position in a phrase or sentence in relation to the noun — e.g., before, after, separated by a verb

Students have a good grasp of sentence and paragraph mechanics. As a group, however, they do not use many adjectives and adverbs in their writing. This lesson on adjectives will be followed by lessons on using adjectives in their own writing and by lessons on adverbs.

LESSON SET-UP

Signal for attention: Make "peace" sign.

Statement of behavior expectations: Clear desks; eyes on me; mouths closed. Point out red stop sign at front of room which means this is a "raise hand and wait to be called on" lesson. **(diversity strategy)**.

LESSON OPENING

Say: "I'm going to read you two passages that sound very different. Listen carefully and see which passage you think is the most interesting." Read two passages. They describe students in this class and the school. **(diversity strategy)**

Say: "The reason the second passage sounded much more interesting to most of you is that it contains many adjectives. By the end of today's lesson, you'll know how to identify adjectives in phrases and sentences."

Say: "We first need to review nouns in order to understand adjectives. Turn to your partner. Partner #1 says definition of noun and gives one example from each category — people, places, things. Partner #2 listens. Then switch." **(diversity strategy)**

If necessary, show transparency as review.

<u>people/animals</u>	<u>places</u>	<u>things</u>
women	restaurant	basketball
boy	park	bug
Mr. Jones	Rocky Beach	Volkswagen

LESSON BODY

Note to myself: (1) <u>Selecting examples of nouns</u>: I need to include examples of people, of places, of things, singular and plural, proper and common, of sentences that include more than one noun. (2) <u>Selecting examples of adjectives</u>: I need to include examples from the various categories of adjectives and of sentences where the adjective comes before the noun, after the noun, or separated from the noun by a verb.

(1) **PRESENT EXAMPLES**

Note: All words and phrases throughout the lesson will be read out loud so that students with reading difficulties will be able to follow along. **(diversity strategy)**

Show: Transparency #1, which includes the following sentences and phrases:
1. <u>large, ferocious, golden</u> lion
2. <u>talented</u> Supersonics
3. <u>funny, bright,</u> Michael
4. <u>shiny, sleek, red</u> cars
5. soccer, <u>exciting</u> and <u>fast</u>
6. Mrs. Deeter is <u>old</u> and <u>grouchy</u>.
7. <u>many</u> chairs
8. The <u>beautiful</u> daffodils burst from the ground.
9. <u>intelligent</u> Molly
10. Her <u>fat, lazy</u> dog slept all day.

11. <u>long</u>, <u>black</u> hair
12. His hair is <u>black</u> and <u>long</u>.
13. A <u>thrilling</u> ride on a roller coaster.
14. Gail and Leon, <u>dedicated</u> fans, go to every game.
15. <u>tiny</u>, <u>fragile</u> figurine

(2) SET UP THE DISCOVERIES

DISCOVERY #1 - The definition of an adjective

Say: "Carefully examine the underlined words (adjectives) in the phrases and sentences. See if you can figure out a definition for adjective. Work until you hear me say stop."

Have students talk it over in *table groups*; remind students of table group rules. **(diversity strategy)** Monitor. When most students have figured it out, have them share.

<u>Questions and prompts</u>: If stuck, ask, "Adjectives have something to do with nouns. What is it?" Circle nouns. Draw arrows from adjectives to nouns.

Say: "Stop." Write the definition that students "discovered" on transparency. (See definition in concept analysis.) Be sure that it contains the key phrase "describes nouns."

Use unison responses and have random individuals and whole group repeat definition of adjective. Then have all students copy the definition into language journals. **(diversity strategy)**

DISCOVERY #2 - Categories and examples of adjectives (Refer back to Transparency #1)

Say: "For the next discovery, you'll be doing *partner work*. See if you can figure out various categories of information that adjectives tell about a noun. Based on what you've seen so far, what do you think one category might be?" If needed, do one or two examples together with the whole group; e.g., #15 - tiny and fragile are physical traits.

 "Work to find at least 3 different categories of traits and at least 3 examples of each category. Work until I say *stop*. If you think you have found all possible categories and examples before the time is up, compare answers with another partner group." Partner work - #1 is recorder; #2 is reporter; switch after every three examples.

Note: During partner work, Linda and Patty need to work with Joanne and Gladys.

<u>Questions and Prompts</u>: If stuck and not "discovering" the categories, go back to examples and work together. For example, #11 includes an example of color (black).

Say: "Stop." Call on reporters to share when most have written at least 3 examples of adjectives in at least 3 categories of traits.

Construct a cognitive map on transparency to organize the categories, subcategories, and examples that are "discovered." **(diversity strategy)** Tell students there may be other categories. Be sure to include a good variety. For example, *physical traits* — size; e.g., tall, short, — shape; e.g., rectangular, — color; e.g., green, gold.

Students copy cognitive map into language journals.

DISCOVERY #3 - Position of adjectives in relation to noun (Refer back to Transparency #1.)

Say: "Now see if you can figure out where the adjectives are located in relation to nouns. Work with your *partner* and write a rule that tells about where adjectives are located in relation to nouns and other words." Monitor and listen.

Questions and Prompts: If stuck and not "discovering" where adjectives are located, go back to examples and point out:

    #11 - "Look at the adjective. Is it before or after the noun? Everyone...?"
    #12 - "Look at the adjective in this phrase. Is it next to the noun? What kind of word stands between the adjective and the noun?"

Say: "Stop."

Write the rule students "discovered" on transparency. Have students read the rule in unison *and* have them copy definition into language journals.

(3) SUPERVISED PRACTICE WITH FEEDBACK

Show: Transparency #2 (new examples) and pass out identical student handout. Students will locate the adjectives and circle them.

Note to myself: I may only need the individual practice activity *but* whole group and small group are included *just in case!*

Optional whole group practice — Do first 3. Various students come up to overhead and circle adjectives. Other students hold up agree/disagree cards which are kept in their desks.

Optional partner practice — Do next 4 with *partners* (recorder/reporter). Monitor.

Mandatory individual practice — Do next 3 individually. Monitor. If students are ready, go to closing.

LESSON CLOSING

Review today's learning with students — definition of adjectives; categories and examples of adjectives; position of adjectives in a sentence.

EVALUATION

Have students finish circling the adjectives in the phrases and sentences #10-20 independently.

Say: "Work independently. If you need help reading any of the words, ask your partner." Remind students to put the finished paper in the basket; to use the rest of period for study hall.

Note: I am choosing not to directly test the students on defining and categorizing adjectives. I am only interested in those skills as they relate to helping students identify adjectives and eventually use more adjectives in their writing.

EXTENDED PRACTICE

Tomorrow, the morning opening activities will include additional practice with identifying adjectives.

EDITING TASKS

specific management strategies:
Remind students about partner rules. Roles of recorder and reporter were taught earlier in the year and are used routinely.

individual accommodations:
Have Marlene read the sentences to Kay, if needed.

materials/equipment:
- two reading passages
- transparencies #1 and #2 - examples of phrases and sentences
- handouts - identical to transparency #2
- 3" X 5" cards - agree written on one side, disagree on the other.

Chapter 10

Concept Teaching - A Special Case

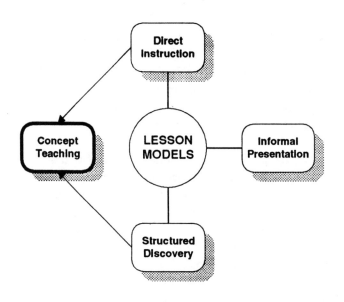

INTRODUCTION

Concept teaching is a special case because it is not a separate model of teaching. It is the content of this type of lesson that differs, not the instructional approach. Either direct instruction or structured discovery models may be chosen to teach concepts. Concept teaching is a separate section because the planning decisions required are specialized.

CONCEPTS DEFINED

Concepts are categories of knowledge. For example, "island" is a concept. There are many specific examples of islands; e.g., Orcas, Oahu, Bermuda. They all belong to the category of island

because they have certain attributes in common — i.e., a land mass completely surrounded by water. Teaching concepts is much more efficient than solely teaching specific examples (Cummings, 1990). A geography teacher does not need to teach every island in the world separately because learning concepts allows us to generalize. If the concept of island is understood, new places can be recognized as being islands if they have the necessary traits.

To check your understanding of "concept," consider the following examples and nonexamples:

Examples	Nonexamples
- president	- Bill Clinton
- rocking chair	- my grandma's black rocker
- Impressionist art	- Van Gogh's "Starry Night"
- planet	- Mars

To determine if something is a concept, ask if you can think of more than one example of it. In other words, planet is a concept because there are several examples of it — Mars, Venus, Jupiter, and others. Mars is not a concept because there is only one Mars. Other examples of concepts are triangle, continent, justice, monarchy, fruit, reptile, and heavy.

TYPES OF CONCEPTS

Concepts vary according to how concrete or abstract they are; how broad or narrow they are, and the type of definition they have. It is important to think about the type of concept to be taught when deciding how to teach it.

Some concepts are very concrete — e.g., table, flower. Some are very abstract — e.g., truth, love. Many fall in between — e.g., polygon, family, adverb. The more concrete a concept is, the easier it is to learn and to teach.

Some concepts are very broad — e.g., living things. Some are very narrow — e.g., elephants. Between these two extremes, there are a series of concepts in a hierarchy, as in the following example:

living things → animals → mammals → land mammals → large land mammals → large land mammals living today → elephants.

When teaching a particular concept, it is important to fit it into a hierarchy of broader and narrower concepts. For example: "We have been learning about geometric shapes. Today we are going to learn about one type of geometric shape - the triangle. In later lessons we will learn about different kinds of triangles; e.g., equilateral triangles."

Typically, a very narrow concept should not be taught — e.g., "elephant" — through a formal concept lesson. (Unless, perhaps, the students are training to be wildlife biologists.) There are many, many concepts, and it is necessary to select those which are most important and useful for the students to learn.

Concepts also vary according to how they are defined. For example, "table" is defined in terms of *one set* of attributes; i.e., a table has a flat surface *and* at least one leg. This is called a conjunctive concept. Other concepts — called disjunctive — are defined in terms of *alternative sets* of attributes. For example, a citizen is a native *or* naturalized member of a nation (Martorella, 1994, p. 161). A strike in baseball is a swing and a miss *or* a pitch in the strike zone *or* a foul ball (Arends, 1994, p. 282). A third type — relational concepts — are defined in terms of a *comparison*; e.g., "big." A mouse is big in comparison with an ant,

but it is not big compared to a dog. The concept "big" has no meaning except in relation to something else.

As you analyze a concept and select examples or nonexamples in preparation for teaching, it is important to recognize whether you are teaching a conjunctive, disjunctive, or relational concept.

KEY PLANNING CONSIDERATIONS

Concept Analysis

A careful *concept analysis* is essential to effective concept teaching. A concept analysis includes a definition, critical and noncritical attributes, and examples and nonexamples of the concept.

Defining the Concept - Developing a definition at an appropriate level for the students is important. Dictionary definitions are not always the best to use. A better source may be the glossary of content area textbooks. The language and complexity of the definition must be suitable for the students. For example, the definition of "mammal" or "square" would be stated differently for first grade students than for tenth grade students.

Listing Critical and Noncritical Attributes - When a concept is analyzed, critical and noncritical attributes — those which will be most helpful in distinguishing that concept from similar ones — must be listed. Critical attributes are essential characteristics of a concept. For example, "four sides" is a critical attribute of a square. However, when defining a concept, any one critical attribute is necessary but not sufficient to defining the concept. A square must have four sides, but the sides must also be of equal length. Noncritical attributes of a concept are those which are not necessary. Whether the length of those equal sides is three miles or three inches is unimportant. Size is a noncritical attribute of a square. A square is a square whether it is big or small.

Selecting Examples and Nonexamples - Examples and nonexamples must be carefully selected to bring out all of the critical and noncritical attributes of the concept. It is important to begin with the "best" examples; i.e., examples that are the clearest and least ambiguous. Gradually introduce examples and nonexamples which are more difficult to differentiate. For example, do *not begin* with a platypus as an example of a mammal or with a rhombus as a nonexample of a square (Howell, Fox, & Morehead, 1993).

Many examples and nonexamples are needed. That is because different sets are to be used for the initial presentation, for the practice, and for the evaluation.

Opening

When opening concept lessons, it is very important to assess what students already know about the concept and to find out if students have any misconceptions about the concept. Brainstorming or "think to writes" — e.g., write down everything you know about reptiles in two minutes — may be useful. These strategies can also be used to help students connect the new learning with prior knowledge. When possible, help students make connections to personal experience. For example, if you are going to teach the concept "democracy," ask about the students' experiences in electing the class president. Some type of organizer should, also, be used which shows the relationship of the concept being taught to broader and narrower concepts or to related concepts; e.g., islands and peninsulas.

Choosing the Model

Concepts may be taught using the direct instruction model or the structured discovery model. The direct instruction model uses a deductive approach while the structured discovery model uses an inductive approach. Each model requires different steps initially. However, the last two steps are the same in both models.

Direct Instruction Model

- Teacher (T) names and defines the concept.

- T states the critical and noncritical attributes of the concept while showing examples and nonexamples of the concept.

- T provides new examples and nonexamples and asks students to discriminate between them.

- T asks students to explain their answers; i.e., to refer to critical attributes present or absent.

Structured Discovery Model

- Teacher (T) names (usually) the concept.

- T shows examples and nonexamples.

- T asks students to examine the examples and nonexamples and to identify critical and noncritical attributes.

- T asks students to define the concept or explain the concept rule.

- T provides new examples and nonexamples and asks students to discriminate between them.

- T asks students to explain their answers; i.e., to refer to critical attributes, present or absent.

The advantages of the direct instruction model for teaching concepts are that there is less opportunity for confusion or misconceptions and that it is more time efficient. This model is useful when students have little prior knowledge of the concept.

The advantages of the structured discovery model are that this approach may be more interesting or motivating to students and that it provides practice in inductive thinking skills. This model is useful in helping students refine their understanding of

111

familiar concepts.

Students typically have some prior knowledge and experience of a concept before it is taught. It is helpful to assess and to build on each student's knowledge. Also, it is important to ascertain whether the student has formed inaccurate concepts because of limited experience; e.g., all people who speak Spanish are from Mexico; all fruits are edible; all islands have people living on them.

Both direct instruction and structured discovery models are effective for teaching concepts. Each model has advantages. First, determine the concept to teach and write the objective. Then, weigh the advantages of both models. Select the one that best meets the needs of the students.

* *

Figure 10.1 WRITING A CONCEPT TEACHING LESSON

The content of the components below is what would typically be included in a concept teaching lesson plan. When you write your plan, clearly label each component — e.g., Component 1 - Preplanning Tasks — and component parts — e.g., task analysis, objective.

Component 1 - <u>PREPLANNING TASKS PHASE ONE</u>

The preplanning tasks section is a cover sheet for the rest of the lesson plan.
<u>Write</u>:

✎ a *concept analysis*. The concept analysis includes the concept name, definition, critical attributes, noncritical attributes, examples, and nonexamples.

✎ an *objective*. Possible objectives for concept lessons may include the following: (1) define the concept; (2) list critical attributes of the concept; (3) recognize examples and nonexamples; (4) state why something is an example or nonexample of a concept; (5) produce examples; (6) state similarities and differences between related concepts; (7) use the concept in a novel way; or (8) produce a diagram of the concept.

✎ an *objective rationale* to help clarify the value of the objective. Some questions are: "Is this an important and useful concept for students to learn?" "Does this concept need to be taught formally as a lesson (e.g., mammal), or does it make more sense for students to informally and gradually learn the concept through experience (e.g., pet)?" Is it important that students memorize a definition or list of attributes as long as they can discriminate between examples and nonexamples?"

▸ Determine the lesson model to use; i.e., direct instruction or structured discovery.

▸ Think about the lesson process and diversity strategies to be included.

Component 2 - <u>LESSON SET-UP</u>

The *lesson set-up* is the first component of the lesson plan that is actually presented to students.
<u>Write</u>:

✎ a *signal for attention* — e.g., "5, 4, 3, 2, 1" or "1, 2, 3, eyes on me."

✎ a *statement of behavior expectations* — "Ask your group for help before you ask me."

Component 3 - LESSON OPENING

The lesson *opening* should effectively prepare the students for the new learning.

Write:

✎ the lesson opening. When you think how you will **state the objective** and **objective purpose**, consider whether you will be using a direct instruction or structured discovery model. For example, you would not state a specific objective which includes the definition of the concept at the beginning of a discovery lesson.

Component 4 - LESSON BODY

The *lesson body* is a detailed, step-by-step description of the actual teaching to the objective that will be done — i.e., what the teacher and the students will be doing. Be sure to select a variety of strategies which allow for all students to actively respond in many ways; e.g., say, write, draw.

Write:

✎ the lesson body. The sequence of steps in the lesson body will differ depending on which model you have chosen. If you choose the direct instruction model, you will begin by telling the students the concept definition or rule and then presenting examples and nonexamples. If you choose the structured discovery model, you will first present examples and nonexamples and then lead students to discover the concept definition or rule.

✎ diversity strategies throughout lesson body. Options include: (1) When presenting examples and nonexamples, use cues such as underlining, colors, arrows, etc. to emphasize critical attributes. Gradually fade the use of these cues. (2) Be sure to use best or clearest examples until students are sure of the concept. Leave out any extraneous information. Use examples familiar to students. (3) If it is important that students remember several critical attributes, suggest mnemonic devices.

Component 5 - EXTENDED PRACTICE

Extended practice opportunities help students develop high enough levels of accuracy and fluency to ensure that they can generalize the skill or knowledge. Make sure that the practice activities are congruent with the objective. For example, if your objective is that students produce new examples, be sure to provide practice on that, not just on identifying examples in a list which you have provided.

Write:

✎ a plan for providing extended practice following the lesson. Options include: (1) students produce their own examples and nonexamples; (2) students create concept maps or webs; (3) students identify examples of concepts in context; e.g., in passages in textbook; (4) students compare new concept to related concepts.

Component 6 - LESSON CLOSING

The lesson *closing* should effectively tie the lesson together and follow the lesson body or extended practice.

Write:

- ✎ a strategy for closing the lesson. Options include: (1) review the concept definition, critical attributes, and best examples; (2) discuss related concepts or preview future lessons on related concepts; (3) review the purpose of learning the concept; (4) describe how students can use their understanding of the concept in future activities and lessons; (5) ask students to show their work; e.g., concept maps or new examples; (6) refer back to opening; e.g., ask students to add to or to correct their "think to writes."

Component 7 - EVALUATION

The lesson *evaluation* was planned when the objective was written, so the evaluation must match exactly what is stated in the objective. Remember that evaluation is not necessarily a paper and pencil test.

Write:

- ✎ a plan for evaluating whether learning has occurred. It is essential to use new examples when evaluating the understanding of concepts. Otherwise, students may have merely memorized the examples provided in the body of the lesson.

Component 8 - EDITING TASKS

This component provides a way to evaluate and complete the first draft of the lesson plan.

- ▸ Examine each component to make sure all are congruent; i.e., that all match. Rewrite as necessary.
- ▸ Evaluate the use of diversity strategies throughout the lesson. Write in any additional strategies needed for the whole group or for individuals.

Write:

- ✎ specific management strategies needed — e.g., during transitions, during whole group instruction. Consider individual student needs for structure, seating, reinforcement, etc.
- ✎ a list of materials/equipment needed for this lesson. When possible, use real objects, pictures, recordings, etc. as examples in the lesson.

STUDY SUGGESTIONS

1. Review these terms in the appendix:

    concept analysis
    signal for attention
    statement of behavior expectations
    supervised practice
    extended practice
    active participation
    evaluation

2. Read the sample lesson plans at the end of this chapter.

3. Write a concept teaching lesson plan. Topic ideas could include the following: reptiles, Impressionist art, emergencies. Refer to Chapter 5 as well as to Chapter 10.

REFERENCES AND SUGGESTED READINGS

Arends, R.I. *Learning to Teach*. 3rd ed. New York: McGraw-Hill, 1994.

Cummings, C. *Teaching Makes a Difference*. 2nd ed. Edmonds, WA: Teaching, Inc. Chapter 11, 1990.

Howell, K.W., S.L. Fox, and M.K. Morehead. *Curriculum-Based Evaluation: Teaching and Decision Making*. 2nd ed. Pacific Grove, CA: Brooks/Cole, 1993.

Martorella, P.H. *Concept Learning and Higher-Level Thinking*. In J.M. Cooper (Ed.), *Classroom Teaching Skills*. 5th ed. pp. 153-188. Lexington, MA: D.C. Heath, 1994.

SAMPLE CONCEPT TEACHING LESSON PLAN #1

Topic: THE CONCEPT "SQUARE"

This is an example of a concept teaching lesson using the *structured discovery* model.

PREPLANNING TASKS

CONTENT ANALYSIS:

concept analysis:

  <u>name</u>: square

  <u>definition</u>: a closed figure with 4 sides of equal length and 4 equal angles

  <u>critical attributes</u>: closed, 4 equal sides, 4 equal angles

  <u>noncritical attributes</u>: size, position in space, interior or exterior designs

  <u>examples</u>:

  <u>nonexamples</u>:

  cube ⬜ , rhombus ◇

OBJECTIVE: Students will underline 5/5 examples of squares on a page of 10 drawings of various figures.

OBJECTIVE RATIONALE: Knowing the attributes of basic geometric shapes is a prerequisite skill for many concepts in geometry.

LESSON SET-UP

signal for attention: Clapping pattern, students repeat.

statement of behavior expectations: Raise hands and wait to be called on if have questions/comments.

LESSON OPENING

Show: Transparency #1 - examples and nonexamples of squares.

Say: "Today you are going to learn what is the same about all squares and what makes a square different from other shapes. At the end of this lesson, you'll be given a worksheet of shapes that looks something like this transparency. Your 'ticket out the door' will be to select all of the squares."

  "We will soon begin a geometry unit. Knowing the characteristics of various shapes is necessary to understanding basic geometric principles."

LESSON BODY

1. SET UP THE DISCOVERY

Say: "On this side are squares. On the other side are shapes which are not squares. Compare the two groups and think about how all of the squares are alike. Raise your hand when you know one way they are alike." If necessary, cue by numbering the sides on several squares to show there are always four.

Say: "See if you can figure out all of the ways that squares are the same. Discuss your ideas with your partner." Remind students of partner rules and this week's goal to speak at a level that does

not interrupt other students.

Note: Walter will place slash marks on card at his desk contingent on displaying target behavior; i.e., contributing ideas during partner work time.

Monitor partner work by walking around and listening. When most groups seem to have discovered the critical attributes, move on.

2. REVIEW THE DISCOVERY (check for understanding)

Call on nonvolunteers and volunteers to share critical attributes. If necessary, prompt until all are shared. Say: "All of the squares have _____ sides. How many sides do these shapes have... everyone...?

Put up poster with definition and attributes. (**diversity strategy**) Review.

Show: Transparency #2 - new examples and nonexamples mixed together.

Think out loud using the "how to determine if a shape is a square" questions:
— 4 equal sides?
— 4 equal angles (corners)?
— Is this shape closed?
If the answer to all is *yes*, it is a square.

Work the first several for students, then...

3. (check for understanding) Pass out yes/no response cards. Work the next few with the whole group of students. Have them hold up cards and tell *why* or *why not*.

4. (supervised practice with feedback)

Say: "Decide whether or not each of the next 5 shapes is a square and be ready to explain why. When you think you know, discuss this with your partner. Then, I'll ask you to hold up your yes/no card." (**partner practice**)

Say: "Do the last 5 by yourself." Monitor (**individual practice**)

117

LESSON CLOSING

Point out the noncritical attributes — size, position in space, and/or interior and exterior designs. Those do not affect whether or not a shape is a square.

Say: "You'll use the information you have learned about the attributes of a square in the geometry unit we will begin next week. Knowing these attributes will help you make important distinctions between the square and other related shapes."

EVALUATION

See objective. Explain "ticket out the door." Hand out the worksheet described in the objective.

EXTENDED PRACTICE

Students will review/practice information about squares as other shapes and attributes are taught.

EDITING TASKS

specific management strategies

1. This week's goal for partner work is to "speak at a volume level that does not attract the attention of other students."
2. Be sure to give frequent specific feedback to many individuals during this lesson, especially for following directions, remaining in seats, and participating in lessons. **(diversity strategy)**

individual modifications

Walter, contributing ideas.

materials/equipment

1. 23 student response cards - 3 X 5 cards that have yes written on one side and no written on the other. Cards are to be held in front of each student — about shoulder height — so that only I can see the answer; the other students can't.
2. 2 transparencies with examples and nonexamples.
3. 23 copies of "test" worksheet. The following are included:

SAMPLE CONCEPT TEACHING LESSON PLAN #2

Topic: THE CONCEPT "SQUARE"

This is an example of a concept teaching lesson using the direct instruction method.

PREPLANNING TASKS

CONTENT ANALYSIS:

concept analysis:

    <u>name</u>: square

    <u>definition</u>: a closed figure with 4 sides of equal length and 4 equal angles

    <u>critical attributes</u>: closed, 4 equal sides, 4 equal angles

    <u>noncritical attributes</u>: size, position in space, interior or exterior designs

    <u>examples</u>:

    □   ⊡   ■   (□)   ◆   □

    <u>nonexamples</u>:

    ▬   ⌂   ●   ▼   ⊔   ☆   ◗

    cube □ ,   rhombus ◇

OBJECTIVE: Students will underline 5/5 examples of squares on a page of 10 drawings of various figures.

OBJECTIVE RATIONALE: Knowing the attributes of basic geometric shapes is a prerequisite skill for many concepts in geometry.

LESSON SET-UP

signal for attention: Clapping pattern, students repeat.

statement of behavior expectations: Raise hands and wait to be called on if have questions.

LESSON OPENING

Show: Transparency #1 - examples and nonexamples of squares.

Say: "Today you are going to learn what is the same about all squares and what makes a square different from other shapes. At the end of this lesson, you'll be given a worksheet of shapes that looks something like this transparency. Your 'ticket out the door' will be to select all of the squares."

        "We will soon begin a geometry unit. Knowing the characteristics of various shapes is necessary to understanding basic geometric principles."

LESSON BODY

Note: Katherine will place slash marks on the card at her desk contingent on displaying target behavior — i.e., encouraging others — during partner work.

(presentation of information/demonstration)

Show: Poster with critical attributes of a square and Transparency #1 with examples and nonexamples of squares.

1. Go back and forth between the poster and the transparency, thinking out loud the attributes of a square and showing examples and nonexamples.

    A. Say: "All squares have 4 equal sides." Point to examples.
    B. Say: "All squares have 4 equal sides *and* 4 equal angles — corners." Point to examples.
    C. Say: "All squares have 4 sides *and* 4 equal angles *and* are closed." Point to examples. Refer to the poster. Show nonexamples and say what attributes are missing.

Show: Transparency #2 - new examples and nonexamples mixed together.

2. Think out loud using the "how to determine if a shape is a square" questions:
    — 4 equal sides?
    — 4 equal angles (corners)?
    — Is this shape closed?
    If the answer to all is *yes*, it is a square.

Work the first several for students, then...

3. **(check for understanding)** Pass out yes/no response cards. Work the next few with the whole group of students. Have them hold up cards and tell *why* or *why not*.

4. **(supervised practice with feedback)**

Say: "Decide whether or not each of the next 5 shapes is a square and be ready to explain why. When you think you know, discuss this with your partner. Then, I'll ask you to hold up your yes/no card." **(partner practice)**

Say: "Do the last 5 by yourself." Monitor. **(individual practice)**

LESSON CLOSING

Review key attributes. Refer back to the poster. Point out the noncritical attributes — size, position in space, and/or interior and exterior designs. Those do not affect whether or not a shape is a square.

Say: "You'll use the information you have learned about the attributes of a square in the geometry unit we will begin next week. Knowing these attributes will help you make important distinctions between squares and other related shapes."

EVALUATION
See objective. Explain "ticket out the door." Hand out the worksheet described in the objective.

EXTENDED PRACTICE
Students will review/practice information about squares as other shapes and attributes are taught.

EDITING TASKS

specific management strategies
1. This week's goal for partner work is to "speak at a volume level that does not attract the attention of other students."
2. Be sure to give frequent, specific feedback to many individuals during this lesson, especially for following directions, remaining in seats, and participating in lessons. **(diversity strategy)**

individual modifications
Katherine - encouraging others

materials/equipment
1. 23 student response cards - 3 X 5 cards that have yes written on one side and no written on the other. Cards are to be held in front of each student — about shoulder height — so that only I can see the answer; the other students can't.
2. 2 transparencies with examples and nonexamples.
3. 23 copies of "test" worksheet. The following are included:

■ ⊠ ◙ ◇ ▢ ◀◀ ✦ ▢ ◁ ▢

Chapter 11

Using Peers

INTRODUCTION

Why Use Peers

Throughout this book, the emphasis has been on the importance of active student participation in the diverse classroom. Careful and imaginative planning and hard work are required by the teacher so that all students are involved and can obtain success. As the teacher cannot be everywhere at the same time, an abundant source of help can come from students. Having students work with their peers can increase opportunities for active responses and practice with immediate feedback. Using peers may also be motivating, provide practice in social skills, increase social integration, and offer more variety in methods. All of this helps satisfy individual differences and preferences, as well as results in more engaged time.

Examples of Using Peers

There are many ways of having peers work together in activities and lessons. Consider the following examples:

▸ active participation strategies - During informal presentation and direct instruction lessons, students may be encouraged to process new information with peers through techniques such as "tell your neighbor."

▸ diversity strategies - The needs of students with learning or behavior problems may be accommodated by using peer helpers to provide assistance with paying attention, reading directions, homework, etc.

▸ activities - An activity plan may incorporate the use of groups or teams of students for working on projects, solving problems, engaging in discussions, playing games, etc.

▸ supervised practice in lessons - Partner or small group practice may be included as a bridge between teacher demonstrations and individual practice.

▸ extended practice - Ongoing partner practice may be planned, using flash cards for building accuracy and fluency on math facts, for enhancing vocabulary, etc.

▸ structured discovery - Pairs of students or groups may work together to discuss the examples and nonexamples and to discover the concept or rule.

▸ informal presentation - As extended practice, students may form debate teams and prepare arguments based on the information presented.

▸ behavior management - Teams may earn points for quick transitions with students helping and reminding each other of the rules.

Notice that, in all of these examples, partner or group work builds on teacher instruction. It does not replace it.

There are also many formal cooperative learning and peer tutoring programs which can be very effective in the diverse classroom. Some of these may be implemented by individual teachers and some are school-wide programs. *Note:* See the suggested readings at the end of the chapter for information on these methods of using peers.

Potential Problems

Although there are many benefits to using peers, there are potential hazards as well. Simply telling students to work together is rarely enough. Most people have had experience working with others at school or at work when much time was wasted; when one person did all of the work; or when nothing was accomplished. Using peers, like all other teaching strategies, requires (surprise!!!) careful planning. Careful planning is needed so that students do not spend their time chatting, fighting, or exchanging misinformation. Careful planning is needed to avoid chaos as students are forming groups or moving furniture. Students will not necessarily know how to work together — how to cooperate, to share, to listen, to encourage, or to challenge each other. It is important that procedures are established and communicated and that necessary cooperative social skills are assessed and taught.

PLANNING FOR USING PEERS

When to Plan

The time and effort that a teacher spends planning for using peers depends on how they are going to be used. If the intention is to use peer partners or groups often during teaching — e.g., as an active participation strategy; as part of supervised practice; as a regular part of the reading or math or spelling program — then it is most efficient to plan and teach direct instruction lessons on the procedures in advance. That time will be well spent because it will help avoid more planning and teaching time later. For example, in plans for reading lessons, you may simply write: "Find your reading partner and follow the oral reading routine." That will be sufficient if students have previously been taught the routine and have

established partners. If you teach and provide practice on using the "Numbered Heads Together" procedure, then, in activity and lesson plans, you only need to write "Form your Heads Together groups, count off, and discuss..." (Kagan, 1990).

In some cases, the planning will be for the use of peers as a one time event. For example, suppose you are planning an inquiry activity in science. You plan the membership of the groups, the meeting places for the groups, and the procedures for the groups to follow — just for that particular activity. In that case, you would write detailed directions into the "activity middle" component of the activity plan.

Planning Decisions

Regardless of when the plan for using peers takes place, it is always necessary to make decisions about why, how, who, and where.

Think About
— the reason for using peers
— the size of groups
— how tasks will be shared
— the prerequisites
— who will work together
— the management and logistics

The following suggestions are adapted from Arends, 1997; Johnson, Johnson, and Holubec, 1991; and Slavin, 1995.

The Reason for Using Peers in a Lesson or Activity

What purpose does it serve? Do not assume that using peers is always superior to individual work. It is necessary to think through the reason for using partners or small groups. For example, in an activity, the benefits of having students work on group projects rather than on individual projects might be the following: to generate more ideas; to provide the opportunity for individuals to study one topic in depth; and to provide practice on cooperative social skills. The rationale for using peers as part of supervised practice might be to provide additional support for students' initial attempts at a new skill in order to bring about a higher success rate. Be sure that all students involved in peer practice will benefit from it.

The Size of Groups

Decide which is preferable to use — pairs of students or small groups. Small group size typically ranges from three to six members. There are several factors to consider.

1. **The larger the group, the more cooperative social skills are needed.** It is easier to share materials, to take turns, or to reach consensus with one other person than it is with five other people. Also, in larger groups, equal participation is more difficult to achieve. The decision about group size, therefore, should be partly based on the level of cooperative skills the students have.

2. **All groups do not necessarily have to be the same size.** Diversity can be accommodated by having some smaller and some larger groups. This may need to be done anyway, depending on the total number of students in the class. For example, if you have 23 students, you can form 5 three member groups and 2 four member groups.

3. **The type of task may influence group size.** If students are to take turns reading aloud, then putting students in groups of two means that each student will get more practice than in groups of three or more. If the task is a project where each student has something different to do and all tasks can be done at once — e.g., each student is researching a different topic — then larger groups may be appropriate.

4. **The task may logically divide itself.** Peers may be divided by needed roles — e.g., a

reader and a writer — or according to the content — e.g., reporting on the three branches of government.

5. **Time is a factor.** Typically, the larger the group, the more time will be needed. For example, if the students are to discuss or solve problems together, then more time will be needed for larger groups in order that each member gets a chance to contribute.

6. **Sometimes more mundane elements must be considered.** Group size may be affected by the number of materials or equipment available, the size of tables, etc.

How Students Will Share Tasks

It is important to think about what each student will do during the partner or group work and to communicate this to the students. It is usually not enough to simply tell students to work together, to cooperate, to help each other, to teach each other, or to discuss. It is essential to be much more specific. For example, for partner practice on vocabulary, you might say, "Partner #1 will define the first word and Partner #2 will use it in a sentence; then switch for the second word."

The teacher may think about the typical roles needed in partner or group work, such as reader, recorder, checker, encourager, and timer. Then he or she may decide which roles are needed in a particular task. It is most efficient to directly teach those roles which will commonly be used, so all students know how to carry them out. It is also necessary to decide whether roles will be assigned by the teacher or by the group.

If it is difficult to figure out what each student will do, ask yourself whether this is a task that can be shared and/or whether the size of the group is appropriate. Remember that not all learning is best done in group situations.

Prerequisite Skills and Knowledge

In addition to analyzing whether students have the necessary content knowledge and skills, it is essential to analyze whether they have the required interaction skills — i.e., cooperative social skills — in order to be successful at the task. The following are some examples:

1. Practicing summarizing paragraphs with a partner would follow teacher instruction on summarizing. In that case, you would know that all students have the necessary preliminary content knowledge — i.e., know how to summarize. However, you would also need to decide whether students have the skills to listen to each other, to accept criticism, to take turns, etc.

2. Before you planned to have students discuss a particular topic in small groups, you would decide whether they knew enough about the topic — i.e., had the necessary information or knowledge — to make a discussion productive. You would also need to analyze the students' discussion skills — e.g., making relevant comments, criticizing ideas rather than the person, asking for clarification.

3. Having students form groups and pick a subject to investigate would require that they have the necessary research skills. However, it also requires skills in offering ideas, reaching consensus, etc.

If students do not have the prerequisite cooperative social skills to be successful at the task, there are several options. The problem could be avoided by changing the lesson or activity in order to eliminate the use of peers. The task could carefully be structured to help students be successful — e.g., provide clear and specific directions, change the group size, assign specific roles, etc. The necessary social skills could also be pre-taught. Teach social skills using the direct instruction model. Have students practice by role playing.

Who Will Work Together

The teacher may sometimes choose to form groups at random or to allow students to decide. More typically, he or she will want to plan the membership of pairs and groups carefully. When students will be working together for more than brief periods of time — e.g., for a one hour science experiment — or over longer time periods — e.g., with reading partners for a month — consider the following factors when planning who will work together:

1. **Skills** - Whether homogeneous or heterogeneous pairings or groupings make more sense depends on the task and the purpose. For example, if the intention is to individualize the content of the tasks; e.g., some students need to practice addition facts; some are working on multiple digit addition; and some are working on multiplication, then homogeneous pairs may be chosen so that both students are getting practice on the skills they need. On the other hand, if all students are practicing the same skills, then pairing high achievers and low achievers may make sense. In that way, the low achievers have the benefit of explanations and help from a student who is skilled at the task. Additionally, the high achievers have the benefit of reinforcing their learning by giving those explanations. When forming pairs and groups, it is important to consider study and interaction skills in addition to academic skills.

2. **Compatibility** - It is necessary to consider how students get along together when forming pairs and groups. Students should not be put together who actively dislike each other or who distract each other unless the purpose is to provide practice on conflict resolution or on ignoring distractions.

3. **Integration** - Another consideration in forming pairs and groups is that of promoting social integration. Mixing boys and girls, individuals with and without disabilities, and students

125

from varied cultural backgrounds can increase tolerance and promote friendships in the classroom. However, the teacher must carefully plan for this outcome.

When students will be working together briefly, as in active participation strategies, it makes sense for students who sit near each other to be grouped together. Students should be taught who their "neighbor" is — e.g., the person to their left — and who is included in their small group. If desks are in rows, plan for odd numbers and for the person at the end of the row when thinking about partnerships. Think about and teach students how to turn or move their chairs to form small groups. (*Note*: You will not want much furniture moving for brief group work.) If desks are in clusters or students sit at tables, partners may be designated by the teacher. If peer practice is to be used often, that should be a consideration when seating plans and desk arrangements are made.

Management and Logistics

There are many management, logistical, and organizational issues to consider when students work with their peers. Of course, issues will vary, depending on what students will be doing. The following are some management basics for which planning is essential.

1. **Plan where pairs/groups will meet.** If students are to work together, they will need to be physically close together. If this involves changing seats and/or moving furniture, careful planning is needed in order to avoid too much wasted time. (*Note*: Teaching a lesson on how to move into groups may be time well spent.) No one should be physically excluded from the group, and everyone should be able to see the materials and each other. The pairs/groups should be situated far enough apart so that groups do not distract each other and so they can be easily monitored.

2. **Plan how to regain attention.** When students are working and talking together, it can be

difficult for them to shift their attention back to the teacher. They may not easily see or hear the teacher. Therefore, he or she should consider using a stronger *signal for attention* — e.g., a bell — and providing practice in responding quickly.

3. **Plan specific rules for partner or group work.** These will depend on the needs of the students. Specific rules may need to be set regarding staying with the group; how to resolve conflicts; how to correct errors politely; what to do when finished, etc. Students may be required to ask for help from each other before asking the teacher.

4. **Plan how you will monitor the partners or groups.** Plan how you will help with both the academic and social tasks of the group. Set goals for yourself. Do not just wander. What are you looking for or listening for?

5. **Plan how you will communicate the procedures for working together to the students.** Remember what has been learned about giving directions clearly and efficiently. The following are some suggestions.

   ▸ List groups and their members on a transparency or chart for students to read.

   ▸ Display a diagram/map or put signs up in the room in order to show where groups meet.

   ▸ Demonstrate how to move desks/chairs, if that is necessary.

   ▸ Show and tell how students should work together — e.g., demonstrate taking turns, reaching consensus, etc.

   ▸ Provide a list of the steps to follow to complete the assignment.

   ▸ Tell students the individual and group objectives, the time lines, and the evaluation procedures.

SUMMARY

Having students work with partners or in small groups during lessons and activities is a strategy with many potential benefits. However, careful planning is needed to ensure that students work together effectively and efficiently. Planning is necessary in order to determine the size and membership of groups; to decide how students will share tasks; to evaluate the knowledge and skills needed by students; and to figure out how to manage the classroom.

* * * * * * * * * * * * * * * * * * * *

REFERENCES

Arends, R.I. *Classroom Instruction and Management.* New York: McGraw-Hill, 1997.

Johnson, D.W., R.T. Johnson, and E.J. Holubec. *Cooperation in the Classroom.* Edina, MN: Interaction Book Company, 1991.

Kagan, S. *Cooperative Learning.* San Juan Capistrano, CA: Resources for Teachers, 1990.

Slavin, R.E. *Cooperative Learning: Theory, Research, and Practice.* 2nd ed. Needham Heights, MA: Allyn and Bacon, 1995.

SUGGESTED READINGS

Greenwood, C.R., L. Maheady, and J.J. Carta. "Peer Tutoring Programs in the Regular Education Classroom." In G. Stoner, M.R. Shinn, and H.M. Walker (Eds.) *Interventions for Achievement and Behavior Problems.* pp. 179-200. Silver Spring, MD: The National Association of School Psychologists, 1991.

Jenkins, J. and L. Jenkins. "Peer Tutoring in Elementary and Secondary Programs." *Focus on Exceptional Children. 17.* pp. 1-12, 1985.

Johnson, D.W. and R.T. Johnson. *Teaching Students to Be Peacemakers.* Edina, MN: Interaction Book Company, 1991.

Slavin, R.E. *A Practical Guide to Cooperative Learning.* Needham Heights, MA: Allyn and Bacon, 1994.

Utley, C.A., S.L. Mortweet, and C.R. Greenwood. "Peer-Mediated Instruction and Interventions." *Focus on Exceptional Children. 29.* pp. 1-23, 1997.

Glossary/Explanation of Components

ACTIVE PARTICIPATION - Active participation means that all students are responding by talking, writing, or doing something overt, which is directly related to the lesson or activity. By using active participation strategies, students are kept engaged, and it is more likely that they will learn and retain new information. These strategies also allow the teacher to *check for understanding* early and often. Most lessons and activities eventually involve all students in active practice or processing of some sort. However, it is very important that students are asked to actively respond right from the start — e.g., during the presentation of information segment of a direct instruction lesson.

STRATEGIES

1. Ask for unison responses from the whole class or from rows or groups. Say, "The name of this river is... Everyone?" Make sure that everyone is, in fact, responding.

2. Ask everyone to write down an answer on paper, on a small blackboard, on a dry-erase board, or on a magic slate and then tell them to hold it up so you can see it. For example, tell everyone to write an adjective that describes a chair.

3. Ask students to respond through hand signals. Say, "As I point to each number, put thumbs up if you would round upward..."

4. Ask students to respond using student response cards or other objects. Say, "Hold up the green card if the word is a noun." or "Hold up the isosceles triangle."

> Strategies 1-4 work well when the questions require brief answers. They allow you to check the understanding of all students and provide many opportunities for the students to respond/practice in a variety of ways.

5. Ask a question, and then ask students to say the answer to their neighbor or ask partners to take turns summarizing, defining terms, or giving examples.

6. Ask a question, ask students to think about the answer, and then discuss the answer with their neighbor. Call on pairs to share their answer — e.g., Think - Pair - Share (Lyman, 1992).

7. Ask a question, and then ask students to share and discuss their answers in small groups — e.g., Buzz Groups (Arends, 1997), Numbered Heads Together (Kagan, 1990). It is important to keep the groups accountable for involving all members. For example, you may ask that all answers be recorded, or that groups defend their method of reaching consensus, or you may pick one student at random to speak for the group.

Strategies 5-7 work well when you are looking for long and varied answers. They also are effective when many students are eager to speak, but there is not enough time to call on each student individually. Students who are uncomfortable speaking to the entire class may readily speak to a neighbor or small group.

ACTIVITY GOAL - The activity goal is stated as part of the preplanning tasks section of an activity plan. When you clearly state what you plan for the students to gain from the activity, an activity goal is provided. The goal may be broader and/or less specific than a short term objective; e.g., "Students will be familiar with current events." The goal may also be written as a specific objective, but generally the students may not be expected to reach it for a number of weeks or months. For example, "Students will state personal opinions on current event issues and provide data from at least three sources to support those opinions."

ACTIVITY RATIONALE - The activity rationale is the preplanning task which involves writing a justification for the activity goal. This task requires thinking through carefully why students need to do the activity. Rationales such as "I thought it would be fun." or "I happen to have this video tape." are definitely questionable. Activities ought to be fun and motivating, of course, but they also need to result in important learning. Consider the following examples.

▸ goal = Students will state a personal opinion on current event issues and provide data to support that opinion. rationale = It is important that students understand that opinions have more value when they are backed up with facts.

▸ goal = Students will learn all addition facts. rationale = Knowledge of addition facts is essential for accuracy and fluency in all addition computations.

ADVANCE ORGANIZER - An advance organizer is a picture, a diagram, or a statement made by the teacher just prior to the presentation of the new information and/or materials (Arends, 1997, p. 274). It is more abstract than the content of the current lesson and provides students with an organized way to think about the information to be presented. During a lesson opening, a teacher may use one strategy to address prior knowledge — e.g., a review of previous related lessons — followed by the presentation of an advance organizer. While an advance organizer may help students utilize their prior knowledge, it should be designed to relate directly to the information that follows it.

CHECK FOR UNDERSTANDING - It is necessary to set up opportunities during lessons and activities to monitor whether or not the students are grasping the desired learning. A check for understanding is the monitoring opportunity. Use of *active participation* strategies help make a check for understanding more reliable because students respond <u>overtly</u> in some way. Answering questions verbally; showing thumbs up or thumbs down in response to questions; writing information on a piece of scratch paper; and holding up a response card are examples of overt responses that could help monitor for student understanding and progress during a lesson or activity. Checks for understanding should be done early in both lessons and activities and continued at appropriate times throughout — e.g., when directions are given. These should be noted directly in the written plan.

CLOSING - The closing is an ending to a lesson or activity. All lessons and activities should include a closing which gives students one more opportunity to review the learned material. The closing can help create a smooth transition from one lesson or activity to the next. It may include one or more of the following.

1. a review of the key points of the lesson or activity — e.g., after reading a short story to her students, Mrs. Meurer reviews major accomplishments of the life of Martin Luther King, Jr.

2. opportunities for students to draw conclusions — e.g., Mrs. Vossbeck helps students examine the relationship between lack of supervision and juvenile crime.

3. a preview of future learning — e.g., following an activity designed to create interest in an upcoming unit on the solar system, Mr. Maberry gives a brief explanation of unit lessons and activities that will occur in the next few days.

4. a description of where or when students should use their new skills or knowledge — e.g., Mrs. Weidkamp reminds students to try out their new social skill at recess.

5. a time for students to show their work — e.g., Mr. Isom has students share the three dimensional shapes they constructed during the math lesson.

6. a reference to the lesson opening — e.g., Mrs. Howell restates the lesson objective as she prepares to distribute the evaluation portion of her lesson.

CONCEPT ANALYSIS - It is important to do a concept analysis prior to concept teaching. This type of *content analysis* helps the teacher think through and write down exactly how the essential elements of the concept will be explained. A concept analysis includes: a definition of the concept; a list of critical attributes which are distinguishing features or characteristics; a list of noncritical attributes; a list of examples; and a list of nonexamples. It is sometimes helpful to list related concepts as well.

Example
concept name: consonant digraph
definition: two consonant letters representing a single speech sound
critical attributes: two consonant letters; one sound
noncritical attributes: position in word; adjacent letters
examples: show, faith, chop, elephant, rang, rough, school
nonexamples: start, asking, crop, wasp, plant, burger, split
related concepts: vowel digraphs, consonant blends

CONTENT ANALYSIS - Content analysis is a broad term that refers to a variety of ways to think about and plan the content to be taught. It is a valuable, necessary preplanning task. A thorough content analysis could consist of any of the following: a *subject matter outline*, a *task analysis* or *concept analysis*, a list of *key terms/vocabulary* and definitions, and/or a list of *prerequisite skills/knowledge*.

The type of content analysis to do depends on *what* is being taught. For example, when the plan is to teach a concept, the content analysis will always be a concept analysis. When the plan is to teach a skill or procedure lesson, a task analysis would always be used. A subject matter outline works best for organizing information. All lessons may have key terms/vocabulary that need to be defined in ways the students would understand. Determining prerequisite skills/knowledge would also be routinely considered as part of a content analysis. This would help determine the appropriateness of the content and the planning of the objective(s).

DEMONSTRATION - During the body of the lesson, the teacher demonstrates — shows, models — the new knowledge or skill. The demonstration segment can occur before and/or after the *presentation of information*. To demonstrate can mean showing a product — e.g., "This is an example of a friendly letter." — or it can mean modeling a process — e.g., "Watch me as I set up the equipment." or "Listen as I think out loud while solving this math problem." A skit or role play can also be an effective method of demonstrating a new skill. It is important that the teacher or other expert do the demonstrating so that the students have a correct model to follow. Asking students to demonstrate will come later in the body of the lesson. (See *supervised practice*.) Notice that the demonstration is in addition to visual aids and examples used during the presentation of information.

EVALUATION - The evaluation section of a lesson plan is where the teacher writes a clear description of the method that will accurately determine whether or not the students have mastered the lesson objective. The importance of this section seems obvious, yet it is frequently overlooked or addressed as an afterthought. The information gathered through evaluation is what is used to help make sensible planning decisions. It allows the teacher to determine whether he/she should build on the current lesson or whether some or all of the information needs to be retaught.

When the lesson objective was written, the evaluation was also planned. A well written objective contains a clear description of what students will do that will provide evidence that learning has occurred. Consider the following objective: "When shown a blank diagram of a volcano, students will label all parts — e.g., the crust, the magma — correctly." It is easy to "picture" what will be happening during the evaluation of this objective. At the end of the lesson, an unlabeled diagram of a volcano will be passed out, and students will label the various parts. They will be doing the labeling *without* help from anyone — e.g., no "hints" from the teacher; no help from a partner. Remember that evaluation is used to determine an *individual* student's *independent* performance in relation to an objective.

Evaluation is often more complex than that described in the volcano example. The evaluation may occur in steps and/or at various times or locations. This additional information should be explained in the evaluation section of the plan. For example, imagine that you want to teach students to use a reading comprehension strategy. The lesson objective written is "Students will use all steps in the XYZ strategy when reading for information in content area texts." You decide to teach the lesson over two days. The steps of the strategy will be taught on the first day and the application of the steps on day two. The following is an example of how you might think about the evaluation.

"I will not be able to test the objective at the end of the first day because not all of the necessary content will have been taught. I will, however, test to see that my students have learned the strategy steps because, if there is confusion, I will need to reteach rather than go on to the application step. The test completed after instruction on day one will be the strategy steps written from memory."

"I can test the objective following day two because students should have the information and practice needed to successfully meet the objective. The test will consist of my observing individual students performing the overt strategy actions during short content area reading assignments throughout the day."

At times it may also be desirable to include a description of a long range objective and evaluation that relates to the short term objective for the day. The long range objective for the reading comprehension strategy might be "Students will use all steps in the XYZ strategy whenever reading for information in content area texts." Obviously, students could not be evaluated on their use of this strategy when the teacher no longer has contact with them on a regular basis. However, plans should be included to provide ample generalization and review opportunities for the remainder of the school year. This will increase the likelihood that the strategy will be used following this year. Plans are needed to monitor use of the strategy during these times. The teacher may wish to make a note of this plan in the evaluation section of the lesson plan.

Students need to be monitored carefully during the lesson — especially during individual supervised and extended practice — so it can be determined when they are ready to be formally evaluated. Evaluation should occur only when students are ready, which may or may not be when the teacher had planned for evaluation to occur. This definitely speaks to the importance of having a "back-up plan" for when students progress more quickly or less quickly than expected.

When objectives are planned, it should be remembered that evaluation is not necessarily a paper and pencil test. It can take many forms. Learning may be evaluated by asking students to complete worksheets, make oral presentations, answer questions verbally, make products, perform, or participate. Strive for relevance in evaluation methods and look to routinely use a combination of techniques.

A note of caution: Try not to have the evaluation be affected by unrelated skills — e.g., an evaluation technique, such as asking students to create a bulletin board to show their understanding of the life cycle of the salmon, may actually be an evaluation of their artistic or organizational skills.

EXTENDED PRACTICE - The teacher provides students various opportunities to practice the newly learned skill or knowledge until it is mastered. (*Note:* This is not the same as the initial *supervised practice* which may have been included in the body of the lesson.) Initially, this practice may be homework or seatwork assignments, which are evaluated by the teacher and returned to the students. Students, who do not master the new knowledge or skills as quickly as others, are provided with additional practice opportunities. Once mastery is reached, the teacher provides students with opportunities to generalize the information/skill. Review activities help students retain the information/skill over time.

FEEDBACK - The teacher assists students as they learn new information and skills by giving feedback to the students. Feedback refers to statements that are made to students about the accuracy or inaccuracy of their responses. Feedback is sometimes used in combination with praise — e.g., "That's correct! Great!" — for correct responses. Negative feedback for incorrect responses is most effective when it is combined with a statement, an example, or a demonstration of the correct response. Negative feedback is academic and should be delivered respectfully — i.e., it focuses on the lesson content rather than the personality of the student. All feedback should be specific rather than general. For example, "Your definition of photosynthesis includes all key points!" rather than "Nice job!"

Note: Sometimes practicum students and student teachers feel reluctant to give negative feedback because they are afraid it will hurt a student's feelings if she/he is told the answer is wrong. Consider this example: Ms. Rogers is teaching a lesson on nouns. After some initial instruction, she has students brainstorm new examples of nouns. Cindy calls out "sit." Ms. Rogers says, "Well...yes..., that could be a noun" and then calls on Jerome. Ms. Rogers did not want Cindy to feel badly because her answer was wrong, so she gave

Cindy and all of the rest of the students inaccurate information about what she was teaching. Ms. Rogers could have said, "Cindy, that's a great example of a verb. Remember that a noun names a person, place, or thing. Can you think of an example of a noun?" This response would have given Cindy, and the other students, an additional reminder of the definition of a noun.

GRAPHIC ORGANIZER - A graphic organizer is something that is shown to students that can help them better understand the organization and/or relationships among categories of information being presented or gathered. Examples of graphic organizers are concept maps, note-taking guides, diagrams, webs, T-charts, and outlines — complete or partial.

KEY TERMS/VOCABULARY - One type of *content analysis* is to identify and write out the definitions to key terms or specialized vocabulary words that will be used in the lesson. The definitions need to be written in words that the students will understand. It's important to do this in advance so incorrect or incomplete definitions are avoided. It is not as easy as it seems to think up definitions on the spot.

Student dictionaries and textbook glossaries can be good places to start when trying to write a clear definition for a particular term. Generally, though, this is only the first step. Consider this: You are preparing a list of vocabulary words as part of a reading lesson. One of the words is "myth." You locate a dictionary definition that says a myth is "a story rooted in the most ancient religious beliefs and institutions of a people, usually dealing with gods, goddesses, or natural phenomena." Suppose that you write this definition into your lesson plan. The next day, when you introduce the word "myth" to your second graders, you suddenly realize that, not only do they not understand the entire definition, they do not even understand some of the words that make up the definition. Therefore, all definitions need to be reviewed and restated in words the particular students will understand.

Note: Be consistent in the terms you use with students. For example, if you decide to use the term "subtract," do not randomly alternate with "minus" or "take-away." This can be confusing when learning new information.

LESSON BODY - The body of a lesson is the part where the actual teaching toward the objective occurs. It is really the "heart" of the lesson. When a lesson plan is being written, the body would typically contain the most information. When the lesson is being delivered, the body would take more time than any other component. The body is where the differences among models show up most clearly.

LESSON SET-UP - See *signal for attention* and *statement of behavior expectations*.

OBJECTIVE - An objective is a statement of a learning outcome. (See Chapter 3.)

OBJECTIVE PURPOSE - The objective purpose is what the students are told about the value/rationale of the lesson. It is stated in student terms and lets the students know why the knowledge and/or skill they are learning is important to them — e.g., how it will help them in their daily lives or how it will help them in school. Students respond positively when they understand why they are learning what you are going to be teaching. (See *opening*.)

OBJECTIVE RATIONALE - When a teacher actively thinks about and evaluates the importance and relevance of the lesson objective, she/he is defending the objective. After an objective is written, go back to it and ask the following questions: Does this represent an important outcome? Why should my students know how to do this? Why is this information important for my students to know? Does my objective really represent what I want my students to know? For example, do I really care if they can name three types of penguins, or is the purpose actually to practice following directions? If your answers to these questions help you determine that the objective is not relevant, write a new one.

OPENING - The opening is the component where the actual lesson or activity begins. Its function is to help prepare the students for learning. It can include strategies designed to motivate and focus the students and strategies that help students see the relationship between the new knowledge/skill and other learning. Generally, an opening includes both kinds of strategies.

Openings may be simple or highly elaborate. When making decisions about what to include or exclude in the opening, consider variables such as the following: (a) student background, experience, and prior knowledge; (b) prerequisite skills or knowledge; (c) the abstractness or concreteness of the content; (d) whether this is the first lesson or activity in a series; (e) probable student interest and motivation; (f) the amount of time available for teaching.

You can select ideas for openings from the following two main categories. However, stating the objective and purpose should almost always be a part of the opening.

1. Strategies to motivate and/or focus the students:

    a. telling/showing the objective (*state the objective*); describing the evaluation — e.g., telling students that at the end of the lesson, they will write two complete sentences in which adverbs are included and used correctly.

    b. telling the purpose/rationale/importance/application of the lesson or activity objective (*objective purpose*) — e.g., telling students the current math lesson will help them double check the change they receive after a purchase.

    c. using an attention-getting "set" that relates directly to the lesson in order to capture student interest — e.g., jokes, stories, riddles, songs, poems, demonstrations, video clips.

    d. previewing the sequence of activities in the lesson — e.g., telling students they will read and take notes from their texts and then work in cooperative groups to construct a study guide for their upcoming test.

    e. providing a key idea or generalization as an *advance organizer* — e.g., explain that all foods fit into five basic food groups and that each group is a primary source of specific nutrients prior to providing information about specific foods or food groups.

    f. previewing lesson content through a *graphic organizer* — e.g., showing students a concept map of the parts of a paragraph.

g. providing initial examples which are humorous or personalized — e.g., include the names and interests of students in the classroom in initial story problem examples.

2. <u>Strategies to help students see relationships between the new knowledge/skill and other learning</u>:

   a. connecting the learning to personal experience and prior knowledge — e.g., having students brainstorm examples of rhyming words as a way of beginning a lesson on poetry.

   b. reviewing earlier lessons or activities — e.g., conducting a quick review of regrouping in the ones column prior to teaching regrouping in the tens column.

   c. previewing upcoming lessons or activities — e.g., explaining that the vocabulary words being learned in the current lesson will help students understand the story to be read tomorrow.

   d. showing students an outline of the whole unit — e.g., showing students the table of contents that will be used for the packet of information they will assemble during the respiratory system unit.

   e. stating the relationship of the objective to a longer term goal — e.g., explaining how learning conversational skills will help students gain and maintain friendships.

   f. connecting to other subject areas — e.g., explaining that the letter to be written to a local city council member, as part of the social studies lesson, will be written in exactly the same format learned in language arts.

   g. presenting a graphic organizer — e.g., showing a concept map for the unit on test taking skills with the topic of this lesson on multiple choice tests highlighted.

PREREQUISITE SKILLS/KNOWLEDGE - One part of a content analysis is determining prerequisite skills and knowledge. These prerequisites are what students must already have in order to be ready for a particular lesson. Sometimes these would be broad skills — e.g., being able to read is a prerequisite skill for using encyclopedias as a resource when writing reports. Sometimes the prerequisite skills are more specific — e.g., long division requires skills in estimating, multiplying, and subtracting. Other examples include: using adjectives is dependent on knowing about nouns; and being able to prepare food from recipes is contingent on being able to measure ingredients. It is certainly not necessary, nor desirable, to list *all* necessary prerequisites — e.g., read, attend. These would only be important to think about if nonreaders or "nonattenders" are in the class.

PRESENTATION OF INFORMATION - During the lesson body, the teacher tells — i.e., explains, describes, or defines — the information students need to know in order to meet the lesson objective. This information is analyzed when a task analysis or subject matter outline is completed as part of the preplanning tasks component. The *key terms/vocabulary* that were written out in the preplanning tasks component are also explained here. Any explanation that may be complex and/or have the potential to be confusing should be put in writing to help ensure it is complete, accurate, and clear. For example, if you are going to teach your students how to write paragraphs, you would *not* simply write, "Explain each part of a paragraph." This is too brief because the key information you need to emphasize during the lesson is not planned. You would have to rely solely on your memory to ensure that the key information your students need to know is, in fact, presented to them. It can be very difficult to remember all of the key information when you are up in front of a room full of students. You will not want to write every single word you will say to the students either. Something in between is preferable, such as the following.

<u>Topic Sentences</u>
+ usually/not always first sentence
+ give main idea
+ tell what paragraph is about

The information provided in this section of the lesson should be presented in writing — e.g. on a transparency, a blackboard, a poster, or a handout — as well as orally. Other *visual aids* and examples which can add interest and clarity to the presentation of information are pictures, diagrams, models, video clips, recordings, and objects.

PRESENTATION OUTLINE - The presentation outline is an outline that is used in the lesson body of an informal presentation lesson. It is simply the *subject matter outline* that was written as part of the *content analysis* in the preplanning tasks component. It is used to guide the presentation delivery during the lesson.

SIGNAL FOR ATTENTION - A signal for attention is any strategy that is used to gain the attention of the students. It is part of the "activity beginning" and the "lesson set-up" components. Signals can be verbal — e.g., "May I have your attention, please?" "Eyes up here." "Give me five!" — , they can be visual — e.g., lights off/on, mime movements — , or they can be auditory — e.g., clap hands, ring a bell, turn on music. The lesson may be excellent but, if the students are not paying attention, they will not benefit from it. A great deal of instructional time can be wasted when the teacher has to repeat instructions or directions because he/she did not have the students' attention. Following are some suggestions for using signals effectively.

STRATEGIES

1. <u>Teach</u> the students the signal which means they are to pay attention.

2. Explain and demonstrate what attention means — e.g., stop where you are, look at me, listen with your mouth closed.

3. Practice until the group is able to respond to the signal in a specified amount of time — e.g., 15 seconds. Make it fun. Time the students and then challenge them to reduce the amount of time it takes to get everyone's attention — e.g., play "Beat the Clock." Periodically repeat the timing and the practice.

4. Following the signal, the teacher should remain silent. Make the students responsible, giving no reminders, warnings, or nagging.

5. Remember to praise/acknowledge students for learning/performing this skill.

6. Encourage the students to help each other respond to the signal quickly through nudges, whispered reminders, etc.

7. If the students enjoy competition, divide the class into teams which compete against each other in order to see who is the quickest to respond to the signal.

8. Be sure *you* are ready to begin as soon as you have their attention.

9. Make sure you are *not* starting until you have everyone's attention.

10. If, after your best efforts, students remain slow to give their attention, implement natural consequences. For example, "We need to spend 45 minutes on math today. Any time wasted will have to be made up during free time."

STATEMENT OF BEHAVIOR EXPECTATIONS - One of the best ways to prevent behavior problems is to tell students clearly, in specific terms, the rules for behavior during the lesson or activity. As a practicum student or student teacher, you *must* clearly establish expectations for student behavior. Do not assume that, because the students understand and follow the cooperating teacher's rules, they will automatically behave the same way with you. It is important to have rules and consequences clear in your own mind before attempting to communicate them to the students. Consider the following suggestions.

1. Think about your goals for student behavior. Remember that the purpose of rules in the classroom is to facilitate student learning, not to establish obedience and conformity for its own sake.

2. Think about the activity or lesson and what will be happening during it. Does it include teacher presentation, small group work, use of breakable equipment? What behaviors will help the lesson/activity go smoothly, efficiently, safely, and allow everyone to learn?

3. Recognize that you will need to be especially clear about those rules which vary by situation — e.g., talking during tests versus talking during partner work.

4. You will typically need to state your expectations for talking, being out of seat, asking for help, what to do when finished.

5. Think about how you can best communicate the expectations to the students.

    a. Write the statement of behavior expectations in advance, making sure the language is appropriate for the students. Behavior expectations should be stated firmly and directly, but politely.

    b. Be specific. Say, "Ask permission before using someone else's materials." rather than, "Respect others."

    c. State do's rather than don'ts — e.g., "Raise hands." rather than "No talking."

    d. You are likely to have different expectations for different parts of the lesson/activity. Rather than stating them all at the beginning, state them at the transitions — e.g., before you read the story, before doing seatwork, etc.

6. Be sure to follow through with your expectations.

a. Do not state them and then ignore them.

b. Be consistent — e.g., if you stated that students must raise hands, then do not respond to call-outs.

c. Acknowledge/praise students for following the rules. Be specific.

d. Plan ahead the consequences for not following the rules.

STATE THE OBJECTIVE - This is a statement made directly to the students that informs them what they will be expected to know or to do by the end of the lesson. For example, "You are going to learn the difference between reptiles and amphibians." or "At the end of the lesson, I will ask you to circle the amphibians from a list of animals." The statement is made using words that are appropriate to the age and grade level of the students. It may also be appropriate to show the students the objective and have them write it in their notes. (See *opening*.)

SUBJECT MATTER OUTLINE - A subject matter outline is an outline of the specific content to be covered in the lesson. It is one type of content analysis that would be written during the preplanning tasks component of the lesson plan. Subject matter outlines are most always written for lessons designed to teach specific information. The body of the informal presentation lesson consists of a subject matter outline which is called a *presentation outline*. The following format would promote clear organization of the outline.

1. major topic
   A. subtopic
      1. details
         a. additional explanations

Example 1 - This could be a subject matter outline for a series of lessons.

1. Paragraphs
   A. topic sentence
      1. tells the main idea
      2. often the first sentence
   B. supporting details
      1. tells more about main idea
      2. usually two or three details are included
   C. closing sentence
      1. restates the main idea
      2. usually the last sentence

Example 2 - This could be a section of a subject matter outline for a daily lesson.

1. The Four Main Parts of Flowering Plants (the most common type of plant)
   A. vegetative parts
      1. roots
         a. grow underground

   b. absorb water and minerals

   c. some store food for rest of plant

  2. stems

   a. vary greatly among species

   b. support leaves and flowers

   c. carry water and minerals from root to leaves

   d. every stem has terminal bud

  3. leaves

   a. make most of the food the plant needs to live

   b. arranged so much of its surface is in sunlight

   c. network of veins distributes water

SUPERVISED PRACTICE - During the body of the lesson, after the teacher shows and tells the new knowledge or skill, it is essential that students are provided opportunities to practice it under the teacher's guidance or supervision. There are various levels of supervised practice — whole group, partner/small group, and individual. Decide whether to include group practice based on the checks for understanding and on the characteristics of the task itself — e.g., two people cannot share the task of focusing a microscope. The teacher might begin by demonstrating again but this time involving students — e.g., "Let's all do one example together." "What's the first decision I must make...everyone?" The next level of supervised practice may involve asking the students to practice with a partner or in a small group while the teacher monitors and provides feedback. Students must be told exactly how to work together — e.g., "Partner #1 will circle the errors, and partner #2 will correct the errors; then switch roles for the second sentence." The final, *essential* level of supervised practice is individual practice. Every student must have the opportunity to practice the new knowledge or skill by themselves, but the teacher must be present to give immediate feedback.

TASK ANALYSIS - A task analysis is a list of the steps or subskills which make up a skill or procedure. The following is an example.

  <u>Using an Index</u>

   1. Decide on the topic you want to look up.

   2. Think of a key word related to that topic.

   3. Find the index in the book.

   4. Look up the key word in the index using alphabetical order and guide words.

   5. If the word is not in the index, look for a synonym.

   6. Turn to the page number listed after the word.

The most efficient way of conducting a task analysis is to perform the task yourself while writing the steps, including the thinking process you follow. However, there are cases where the process you follow may be different from the process followed by a child or beginner. The task analysis will help you plan the presentation of information and demonstration.

VISUAL AIDS - A visual aid is anything that graphically depicts or assists in demonstrating, explaining, and/or clarifying information to students. Examples of visual aids are posters, maps, working models, pictures, real objects, real animals, real people, photographs, video or television segments or shows, computer enhanced graphics, overhead transparencies, slides, chalkboard writing or drawings, and any *graphic organizer*. There is almost no limit to the number and kind of visual aids available to the imaginative teacher.

* * * * * * * * * * * * * * * * * * * *

REFERENCES

Arends, R.I. *Classroom Instruction and Management.* New York: McGraw-Hill, 1997.

Kagan, S. *Cooperative Learning.* San Juan Capistrano, CA: Resources for Teachers, 1990.

Lyman, F.T., Jr. "Think-Pair-Share, Thinktrix, Thinklinks, and Weird Facts: An Interactive System for Cooperative Thinking." In N. Davidson and T. Worsham (Eds.), *Enhancing Thinking through Cooperative Learning.* pp. 169-181. New York: Teachers College Press, 1992.

SUGGESTED READINGS

on graphic organizers:

Boyle, J.R. and N. Yeager. "Blueprints for Learning: Using Cognitive Frameworks for Understanding." *Teaching Exceptional Children. 29.* pp. 26-31, 1997.

Bromley, K., L. Irwin-DeVitis, and M. Modio. *Graphic Organizers: Visual Strategies for Active Learning.* New York: Scholastic Professional Books, 1995.

on evaluation:

Howell, K.W., S.L. Fox, and M.K. Morehead. *Curriculum-Based Evaluation: Teaching and Decision Making.* 2nd ed. Pacific Grove, CA: Brooks/Cole, 1993.